# RETURNING
# THE SELF
# TO NATURE

# RETURNING THE
# SELF
## TO
# NATURE

———

## UNDOING OUR
## COLLECTIVE NARCISSISM AND
## HEALING OUR PLANET

### JEANINE M. CANTY

SHAMBHALA

Shambhala Publications, Inc.
2129 13th Street
Boulder, Colorado 80302
www.shambhala.com

Cover art: Nata Slavetskaya/iStock
Cover design: Michel Vrana
Interior design: Derek George

9 8 7 6 5 4 3 2 1

First Edition
Printed in the United States of America

Shambhala Publications makes every effort
to print on acid-free, recycled paper.
Shambhala Publications is distributed worldwide by
Penguin Random House, Inc., and its subsidiaries.

LIBRARY OF CONGRESS CATALOGING-IN-PUBLICATION DATA
Names: Canty, Jeanine M., author.
Title: Returning the self to nature: undoing our collective narcissism
and healing our planet / Jeanine M. Canty.
Description: First edition. | Boulder, Colorado: Shambhala, [2022] |
Includes bibliographical references and index.
Identifiers: LCCN 2021052148 | ISBN 9781611809749 (trade paperback)
Subjects: LCSH: Human ecology. | Sustainable development.
Classification: LCC GF21 .C35 2022 | DDC 304.2—dc23/eng/20211223
LC record available at https://lccn.loc.gov/2021052148

*This book is dedicated to Earth and all her beloveds, each and every sentient being. May we remember that we are family, unraveling our dysfunctions, and renewing our bonds.*

# CONTENTS

# PREFACE

Within this moment, I am writing in a rainstorm—a wall of water, complete with thunder and unseen lightning. This moment culminates the writing of this book, a multiyear inquiry of both passion and concern. I adore the words of the author Tyson Yunkaporta:

> What I will say will still be subjective and fragmentary, of course, and five minutes after it is written it will already be out-of-date—a problem common to all printed texts. The real knowledge will keep moving in lands and peoples, and I'll move on with it. . . . You'll move on too.[1]

When taking my courses, often my students will comment on the publication dates of some of our texts, stretching back decades, yet the content is so relevant to this moment. Unfortunately, our ecological crises are not going out of date, yet I am envisioning a time when they will—a time when we have moved into deep healing and change, when we have collectively moved on to lifestyles that repattern back into relationship with the land and all sentient beings.

In the weeks leading up to this moment, the heat and drought too-often present in the western United States caught up to the community I live in, in the foothills of Boulder, Colorado, marked by high dry grasses, stifling heat, and pending fears of wildfires. I have lived out West for almost three decades and have become accustomed to the dryness of midsummer and the eventual coming of the rains. Yet for several summers this pattern has broken, with the rains sometimes forsaking us and the late summer and fall bringing treacherous fires. Perhaps most discouraging, the beautiful mountain air has been replaced with daily ozone warnings to stay indoors. The current pairings of fires, floods, pandemics, climate refugees, homelessness, poverty, fossil fuel pollution, and unbridled inequities often make us feel that Earth has finally forsaken us—she has decided to finally leave the abusive relationship she has been in with us for decades, or even centuries.

This book examines our growing collective narcissism and the damage we have been doing to Earth, which includes ourselves and fellow humans. The seeds for this inquiry were planted from a difficult romantic relationship I had with a narcissist. Many wise teachers see our difficulties as entry points for new learning and eventual healing. Looking at individual narcissism, I noticed how it mirrored the collective narcissism we are engaging in and the damage it is inflicting on the Earth. Over time I came to the insight that by limiting narcissism to a personal problem, we are not looking at our larger and quite ominous issues.

*Tragic optimism* is a term coined by the Holocaust survivor and existential-humanistic psychologist Viktor Frankl, and it embodies our ability to look for meaning during times of immense collective suffering.[2] It is not wishing for something better to manifest without our effort; rather, it is our ability to stay with the suffering in order to learn its lesson. Waking up to the sobering realities of our ecological crisis and the ways in which our individual and collective narcissism have bred this allows us to embark on a search for not only meaning but healing.

# ACKNOWLEDGMENTS

I acknowledge that I am a woman of color with a rich ancestral lineage living on the ancestral lands of the Arapaho, Cheyenne, and Ute peoples. The seeds for this book were laid through a chance meeting with my now editor, Matt Zepelin, at a book release for our mutual colleague David R. Loy at the Boulder Book Store in Boulder, Colorado. What ensued was the invitation to dive deep into an inquiry and create. I express my deepest gratitude to Matt for his continual support, guidance, and collaboration. Thank you to Shambhala Publications, Naropa University, and California Institute of Integral Studies for helping to support this project. Thank you to my parents: my ever-so-smart mom, Carol-Ann Canty, and my forever-endearing father, the late Joe Canty. There are a host of colleagues, friends, and family members who supported me during the creation of this book and in life in general, including: Billy Nowell, Jennifer Weaver, Amy Brummer, Rachel Peters, Victoria Keziah, Kelly (Kjo) Grebe, James Brooks, M. Jennifer Chandler, Belvie Rooks, Carl C. Anthony, Alfonso Montuori, Gabrielle Donnelly, Joanna Macy, Andy

Fisher, Linda Buzzell, Craig Chalquist, Jason Apt, Suzanne Benally, Joe Soecker, Chuck Lief, Vicky Young, Alison Holmes, Laura Sewall, John V. Davis, Dale Asrael, Gaylon Ferguson, Giovannina Jobson, Susan Griffin; and most especially the Thomae family: my incredibly supportive partner, Randy, and his always-cheering-for-me daughters Ali and Chloe, Boston the dog, and even Moxy the cat—with a special bucket of gratitude to Chloe for helping with the indexing. And, as always, the most important acknowledgment is to our sacred Earth and all beings.

# RETURNING
# THE SELF
# TO NATURE

# 1

---

# A NEW UNDERSTANDING
# OF NARCISSISM

When I was a small child, in kindergarten or maybe even in preschool, my mother used to brush my hair each morning, after breakfast, in our dining room. She would ask me to go upstairs and get my brush and then she would take the time to make my hair look nice for the day. At some point, I started thinking that she asked me to get the brush, instead of getting it herself, because each person only had a finite number of movements in their life and she did not want to waste hers on getting the brush. I sassily tried telling my mother that she should get the brush herself. Not surprisingly, this did not go over well. Looking back on this moment, I see how foolish I was with thinking so mechanistically. Clearly this was poor thinking, as physical movement creates a longer life, not a shorter one. Yet as a small child, I was thinking selfishly of my own well-being and even questioning my mother's care for me. Of course, I didn't hold on to my limited-movements idea for very long. In retrospect, I laugh—still with a tinge of shame—at how silly my thinking was at that time.

Reflecting on my story with the brush, I see it as my first conscious moment of being narcissistic. By that I mean not just an impulsive self-centeredness, like a toddler grabbing for some candy, but a deeper worldview in which the self is preeminent. In that moment I was testing out what it was like to put my needs above those of others and to view the world as having scarce resources. Protecting my needs was most important and even took precedence over the needs and feelings of my mother, the person who birthed and lovingly took care of me.

Flash forward a number of years. As a young teenager, I went to summer stock in New England, which was essentially a theater camp. There were kids ranging from late elementary through high school, and we young folks would put on classic kid productions for the larger community while also being part of a bigger theater that had adult productions. We would stay at the camp for weeks to months each summer. I remember one of my last summers there, at age thirteen or fourteen, being in my bunkhouse with six or seven other kids. One of them, a girl I'll call Mara, was one of my good friends and an incredibly talented young actor. During one group conversation, Mara shared that she knew that God existed and that he was putting on a huge production for her. She let us know that God orchestrated the entire world for her, and we were all just characters in a play that revolved around her. In fact, when she left a room, we stopped existing, almost like puppets in a show that are only alive if someone maneuvers them. We were all alarmed by Mara's contention. We tried for a long time to convince her that her views were wrong, but nothing we said changed her mind.

I don't know if anyone else from that day still holds this memory, but it always sticks with me. It was so frustrating to have someone believe that I was not a real human being with feelings and an identity separate from them. From that moment on, I saw Mara as not only self-centered but mentally ill. How could anyone truly believe that they are the most important person in the world?

Flash forward again, this time to adulthood. Apart from tidbits seen in popular media, I was first introduced to narcissistic personality disorder (NPD)—the intensified, diagnostic version of narcissism—in a romantic relationship with a boyfriend that was quite traumatic and ended badly. The relationship was short—a little over half a year—but quite extreme in its highs and lows. I often found myself the recipient of manipulative behavior that was emotionally abusive and increasingly threatening. The relationship started quickly and intensely. My boyfriend showed me excessive adoration, paid me constant compliments, bought me expensive gifts, and made promises to me. Almost immediately we were spending all our time together. These are among the classic signs of what is called *love bombing*, where overwhelming attention is given to the target of someone with NPD.

Within two months the patterns shifted dramatically. My boyfriend caused alienation from my friends and loved ones as he exhibited a need for constant attention, tracked my whereabouts, made me feel insecure with passive-aggressive comments, and let loose with constant outbursts of rage and jealous accusations. When the relationship abruptly and dramatically ended for the third or fourth time, I found myself experiencing extreme feelings of shame, confusion, and powerlessness on top of being heartbroken. I also found myself needing to make sense of the situation in order to heal.

As a professional scholar, I was able to bring my research skills into my personal life, embarking on a long period of research (through reading as well as speaking with therapeutic practitioners, friends, and colleagues). While early in the relationship I had been certain that a personality disorder was involved, it was not until I was exposed to the literature on NPD that I became convinced that my former boyfriend suffered from this.

※ ※ ※

Okay, it is time to pause and make an important disclosure. When my little-girl self told my mom to get the hairbrush so that I would preserve more of my own limited lifetime supply of movements, that wasn't NPD or even serious narcissism—it was the experimental narcissism typical of any young child. I also doubt that Mara from my theater camp has NPD. I did not stay in touch with her after that summer. I think it's likely that the episode I narrated was a temporary narcissistic phase in her self-development, and I anticipate that she is living a healthy, well-adjusted life.

I also cannot unequivocally claim that my ex-boyfriend has NPD. Only a clinical psychologist or licensed mental health professional could do so, and it is a very difficult condition to appropriately diagnose. I am not a psychologist, and while I hold a PhD and teach in the area of ecopsychology, I am not a licensed mental health professional. I tell the story of my former boyfriend to help flesh out the details and convey the intensity of interacting with someone who exhibits strongly narcissistic behavior. Yet my interest in both narcissism and NPD are not for the purpose of diagnosing and/or categorizing individuals. Indeed, one of the main points of this book is that seeing narcissism as an individual problem *is itself a problem.* My experience with someone who I think suffers from NPD exposed me to the startling realization that this illness is widespread and growing.

We live in a society that in many ways has become quite shallow and materialistic. From internet ads, online shopping, social media websites, and reality television to even the mainstream news, we receive constant messages that our individual self is the most important person in the world, and it is our duty to become as successful, beautiful, fit, wealthy, and famous as possible. The importance of duty to others—sharing, looking out for the common welfare—is minimized, and life comes to seem like a competition. We become insecure in our place in the world when we base our self-worth on such shallow ideals and constantly consume things, people, and places to make ourselves feel worthy. Consumerism, in the sense of buying things, is a major factor in this model, but it is also about consuming in other ways, such as always looking for more exciting relationships, jobs, adventures, or experiences rather than working mindfully with what we truly have.

Living in a culture that encourages fixation on the self,

truisms such as "It's important to look out for number one" present as common sense and valid. Yet there are other cultures that are not so self-centered. In general, Indigenous, earth-based, and Eastern traditions focus more on the welfare of the group, while Western cultures focus on the individual. Western cultures, since the onset of modernity, have increasingly viewed people as independent and individual freedom as paramount. While the emphasis on individuality has enabled many important advances and examples of entrepreneurship, its overemphasis has led us to forget that all beings are bound up with one another within a larger system and that to have the healthiest system, we need to take care of one another. Our individualistic tendencies have become distorted within our current culture as the additions of mainstream consumerism, social media, and pop psychology have further accentuated the importance of the self. Our consumer choices, our self-identity, and the ways we communicate our reality have become increasingly fixed on the self. *What products do I need to look good? What things will make me happy? What activities will make me feel better about myself? Who do I want to impress? How many likes can I get on my post? How can I be noticed even more? How do I compare to others? How can I reach the top?* We are living in an age in which we are literally addicted to ourselves.

In a healthy developmental path, a person may show signs of self-centeredness in early stages of life through young adulthood, yet eventually they mature and behave in ways that consider the welfare of other beings. Our culture, however, exhibits what is called "arrested development," wherein a large portion of the population does not mature in this way and instead continues to display high levels of selfishness—narcissism. While people may look physically mature, many of the adults in our society are acting like selfish children.

Narcissism is becoming an epidemic, and one that threatens not just our mental health and our relationships but Earth itself.

## NARCISSISM ON THE RISE

I believe that narcissism has gone beyond an individual phenomenon to something much broader and more collective. A *meme* is a trend or wave of cultural influence. The time has come to ask: Does the narcissism meme in our society reflect something more than the sum of our individual behaviors? Has narcissism actually become a collective phenomenon? Does our collective narcissism endanger the planet? And if so, why? To pursue these questions, we first need to take a closer look at what psychologists mean by "narcissism."

Researchers have documented that narcissism and its more extreme version, NPD, are on the rise in the US.[1] Narcissism is when a person exhibits self-centered behavior—an inflated sense of self that borders on entitlement. In general, it is not a bad thing to have low to moderate levels of narcissism, as this means we have a healthy ego. Clinical theorists, such as Dr. Craig Malkin, speak to a narcissistic scale or spectrum where having too little or too much narcissism is problematic, yet being in the middle of the narcissistic range is quite healthy.[2] The extreme form of narcissism is the mental health classification of narcissistic personality disorder, coined in 1971 by the psychoanalytic theorist Heinz Kohut. Nine years later, NPD was included in the formal handbook of psychiatric disorders, the *Diagnostic and Statistical Manual of Mental Disorders* (DSM).[3]

While narcissists display selfishness and self-preoccupation, people with narcissistic personality disorder take this to a much greater extreme, exhibiting pathology including traits such as a grandiose sense of self, arrogance, very low empathy for others, shamelessness, hypersensitivity to critique (fragile ego), and an overall constant need to feel more special than others. A key pattern is that people with NPD have trouble keeping relationships, and they display problematic thinking, emotions, and resulting behaviors, which can range into the extreme and even dangerous. However, NPD manifests in many different ways depending on gender and personality type (i.e., introvert and extrovert), as well as other influences. The research on NPD varies greatly: some research claims 1–2 percent of the population has the disorder; other research claims that over 6 percent of the population exhibits NPD during their lifetimes.[4] To add to the ambiguity of these statistics, researchers speculate that most people with NPD go undiagnosed, as they often lack the ability to see they have a problem and many therapists and other mental health-care providers have difficulty spotting the disorder correctly.

It is also a challenging disorder to heal. NPD falls into the category of cluster B disorders, a subsection of personality disorders clumped with antisocial personality disorder, borderline personality disorder, and histrionic personality disorder. While all three of the other cluster B disorders are hereditary, NPD, interestingly, is not. In general, this illness stems from early childhood trauma associated with primary caregivers, typically one's parents. In the next chapter, we will look more closely at narcissism and NPD. What is most important to note, for now, is that narcissism and NPD are on the rise in our society.

## FROM VAMPIRES TO VICTIMS: AN ECOPSYCHOLOGY OF NARCISSISM

I find extreme narcissism and NPD quite alarming. Perhaps most distressing is the lack of success the field of psychology has had in helping folks with these conditions. There is so much negative information directed to sufferers of NPD, with popular media labeling them as vampires, stalkers, abusers, and even as evildoers. Much of the popular literature on extreme narcissism is written by people who've had particularly negative experiences with someone with NPD (most often an ex), such as my own, and it tends to demonize the person. There is not an abundance of people who have successfully recovered from NPD, and most often folks, including licensed therapists, tell you to run far away from someone with NPD. If you want to get a feel for what I'm talking about, search the term *narcissistic personality disorder* and simply read what is posted online. Brace yourself—it is quite shocking.

While there is obvious truth in the pain and suffering people with NPD cause their victims, as a person who believes in basic goodness—that at the core of our unconditioned being, we are inherently good—it feels both unethical and unempathetic to simply dismiss people who have the disorder. The body of psychological research on NPD is in its infancy, and years from now, we may look at the way these folks were treated similarly to the manner we once addressed other conditions before we gained more awareness.

I believe that society demonizes NPD sufferers because we attribute their illness to something private and personal to them as individuals. While exploring this phenomenon, I recollected that many Indigenous cultures view a person's mental illness not as a problem specific to them but rather as a sign that something is amiss within the larger community. Hence mental health is situational—reflective of the history, economics, politics, environmental conditions, and a host of other factors that affect a community. It struck me as odd that the rise of NPD was not viewed as a reflection of the painful structure of our society. We have an epidemic of people scarred from their early childhood and who, as a result, often exhibit extreme emotional states. The fact that there are so many people with childhood trauma and living in a culture that is so "me" focused makes it easier to be on the high end of the narcissistic spectrum. To me, NPD seems like a societal problem.

The central point of *Returning the Self to Nature: Undoing Our Collective Narcissism and Healing Our Planet* is to demonstrate how we can move from the selfish, narcissistic orientation of our society to one that centers regard for others and thereby supports the welfare of our larger community and the living systems of our planet. Here, "others" include not only those in our personal relationships but also those in the widening circles of beings we do not know and even the entire Earth. The assumption—and the case I'll be building throughout this book—is that while narcissism appears as a personal pathology, it is a collective issue that extends to human communities and to our treatment of Earth.

※ ※ ※

As I briefly mentioned, my main area of teaching is ecopsychology, a field that looks at how our society's separation from nature has resulted in widespread human pathology, as well as the current ecological crisis. Yes, I know that is a handful—or rather, a headful—to digest. We will look at this idea more deeply in an upcoming chapter. Ecopsychology attributes our separation from nature to our collective history (shifting from earth-based to industrial and technological societies) and our individual histories—the lack of healthy bonding with nature, including other people, that we received as children. As human beings living within Earth, it is incredibly important to remember that we are animals. Much of our Western paradigm keeps us alienated from this realization, placing humans in a special category separate from nature. Yet we are animals living among a vast community of living beings.

When I was diving into the topic of narcissism, I recalled that some of the early ecopsychology writers briefly touched on narcissism as a cause for materialistic overconsumption in US culture. In a groundbreaking essay from 1995, "The All-Consuming Self," the ecopsychologists Mary E. Gomes and Allen D. Kanner (building on the work of the psychologist Philip Cushman) stated, "American consumer habits reflect both the grandiose and the empty side of narcissism. In terms of the arrogant false self, Americans feel entitled to an endless stream of new consumer goods and services."[5] Of course, the various things that we buy are sourced from finite materials from Earth and create an irreversible impact on ecological systems. Our vast consumption is essentially destroying Earth, including ourselves; our sense of entitlement to things—our narcissism—is at the heart of this.

The field of ecopsychology arose over the last few decades with two main goals. One is to make sense of why humans are causing such widespread destruction to the planet. Another is to respond to the environmental movement's need to adopt a psychological approach rather than always operating from a finger-pointing stance that rests upon political tactics. Ecopsychology recognizes the environmental movement needs psychology *and* that our psychological well-being is dependent on our relationship with nature.

Ecopsychology has four major assumptions. First is that Earth is calling for healing. Rising sea levels, forest fires, floods, oil spills, polluted lands and waters, Superfund sites, mass migration, and homelessness—what are these if not the cries of a damaged Earth? The second assumption is that humans are calling for healing. It often feels that most folks within our society are suffering from addictions to drugs, alcohol, consumerism, technology, or codependent relationships. We are also witnessing high rates of depression, suicide, apathy, racism, homophobia, alienation, poverty, and illness. What if we looked at all these sad and painful human phenomena as symptoms of a pervasive underlying problem rather than as merely distinct personal or societal issues? The third assumption of ecopsychology is that the suffering of Earth and humans is interdependent. These sufferings are not separate phenomena—they are part of the same problem. Fourth and final, ecopsychology sees Western culture—and really any culture that is now living under corporate globalization, which unfortunately is most—as ill. The illness or pathology is embedded within the Western paradigm.

From an ecopsychological standpoint, most people within

our Western culture are ill because we no longer have the intact relationships with the natural world that our earth-based ancestors did. As a result, we do not have a deep sense of trust in the world or ourselves, so we often have problems developing an authentic sense of self, forming healthy relationships, and discovering our greatest gifts. In our Western, globalized, corporate reality, we dedicate less and less time to genuine relationship and the nurturing of our unique callings, and we emphasize more and more the separate self, individual achievement, wealth, fame, and vanity. Essentially we collectively suffer from having a poorly developed sense of self. It is no surprise that most of us never develop into mature adults, and even as adults, we tend to fixate on our ego needs. We are bred to become narcissistic, and it is an epidemic in our society.

In the traditional model of NPD, there is the narcissist and there are the targets of narcissistic abuse—those people that narcissists use to make themselves feel special and gain energetic "supply." A typical narcissist has multiple forms of supply from lovers, spouses, friends, and siblings. Many of these people become disposable; the narcissist drops them when they find another form of supply (a new or former relationship), only to pick them up again when other forms of supply wane. The stories of people in relationships with a person with NPD are horrific. You can imagine the kinds of terrible developments that occur in abusive, addictive relationships that are extremely difficult to leave and, even after they have ended, continue to resurface. The victims of narcissistic abuse become disoriented, continually questioning their reality and their ability to be in healthy control of their experiences.

Although I in no way intend to excuse the behavior of extreme narcissists, looking at the problem through an ecopsychological lens reframes it in important ways. NPD and narcissism in general constitute a spectrum of societal problems that derive from our culture's extreme emphasis on the role of the individual coupled with our society's escalating focus on consumerism, social media, and self-entitlement. When framing narcissism as a societal rather than an individual problem, the perpetrator (the narcissist) is no longer the abuser; instead they become a victim of a problematic system. The system itself is the abuser. In framing narcissism in an ecopsychological context, it is our larger society that abuses both people and Earth.

❧ ❧ ❧

Reflecting on my own story with the natural world, I was born in New York City and my family moved to the suburbs of New Jersey when I was an infant. Though I spent time outside, it was in highly human-designed environments. As a young child I was more aware of other people and human-centered experiences. I will always remember the first time I sensed there was more going on in nature: I walked with my older brother and a couple of his friends a few blocks from our neighborhood to a small creek in an undeveloped area. It felt special and wild; it felt different in a way that both comforted and intrigued me. As I grew a little older, I started to notice how much I loved areas that felt wild, such as beaches or nature preserves. It was not necessarily about being somewhere pristine but rather being in a space that felt alive. I also started to notice nature in more mundane spaces. I recall sitting in the backyard during a particularly rough day in my teenage years and closing my eyes and hearing the sounds around me merge in symphonic layers. The experience instilled a sense of preciousness in realizing that there is so much life in the natural world, vastly larger than the human world, and it ripples out in connection. Moreover I, we, are a part of this. By my midtwenties, I always chose to live in forested spaces on the edge of town. While I know it is a privilege, being surrounded by trees, wild animals, big skies, and starry nights brings me much joy and peacefulness.

※　※　※

Our egocentric, consumerist culture did not form arbitrarily. It was built together and symbiotically with our current model of corporate globalization. As you are probably aware, most of the Western world, and much of the larger world, lives under an economic system that requires constant growth. We have shifted our values from focusing on the welfare of others (including nature) to securing greater wealth and success. Moreover, we have moved from more altruistic forms of leadership, including states and countries, to the domination of economics and politics by corporate entities that transcend state and federal boundaries and work on the global level, hence the term *corporate globalization*. We will dive into this more fully in an upcoming chapter. The bottom line for these entities is to always increase their profit margins. To do so, there needs to be a constant increase in consumers and consumer appetites. By causing people to feel insecure through various forms of messaging and systematic pressure, corporations increase our cravings for more goods and services—essentially wealth and power. This drive keeps us focused on a very shallow version of ourselves.

Okay, time for another pause. While reading this chapter, you may have asked yourself whether you are a narcissist. Maybe you didn't, but I would suspect that most of us have seen some of the above patterns in our own personalities. If you are wondering, don't be alarmed; wondering about one's own narcissism is actually quite common. While I was doing the research for this book, I initially questioned whether I too might be a narcissist. In fact, I had to ask several good friends for feedback. All of them quickly dispelled this possibility. One of my best girlfriends wisely told me that just asking this question demonstrated that I was not a narcissist. Yet in truth, most of us, myself included, demonstrate elements of narcissism, both healthy and unhealthy. To use a metaphor, it is as if the stream of corporate globalized culture flows toward self-centeredness. If we swim eagerly with the current, we are likely to develop exaggerated and unhealthy forms of narcissism. And we actually have to swim *against* the current to locate wider, wilder, and more connected versions of ourselves.

This is one of the key points of this book: It is the larger culture, our society, that is breeding us to be narcissistic, and this is a problem. Not only does it cause us to be more self-centered, but it also causes us to not care as deeply for the welfare of others.

## A SENSE OF ENTITLEMENT: ARE NARCISSISM AND RACISM CONNECTED?

In addition to ecopsychology, another central focus of my teaching is social justice. As a woman of color who is deeply connected to Earth, I realized early in my path that social and ecological issues are intrinsically connected, most specifically in their embeddedness in systems of oppression. Throughout this chapter, I have talked about the importance of viewing narcissism as a societal problem rather than simply a personal issue. With introducing ecopsychology, we see that our destructive behaviors toward Earth are connected to our Western, materialistic, me-centered paradigm. Both narcissism and the ecological crisis are directly related to our Western culture. A logical question that emerges is: What about racism? Are narcissism and racism connected, similarly to how narcissism and the ecological crisis are related?

The answer is yes. Our growing culture of narcissism occurs, in large part, due to the heavy emphasis on consumerism sparked by the desires for greater wealth, specialness, and privilege. US society's capitalist-based system encourages ever-increasing prosperity for the individual. Our country's history with racism and other forms of oppression is not a secret, and right now these issues are front and center. We have lived a mythological story that coos us into believing that if we work hard, wealth and security will be within reach. As more and more folks realize that the "American dream" is no longer obtainable—always receding past a horizon of low wages, student loans and other forms of debt, rising real estate prices, and high cost of living—we increasingly question this story. Coupling all this with modern racism, many are learning that this country has been based on systems of white privilege through which the American dream was structured for those who claimed whiteness—first with being white and upper class and eventually becoming more open to working-class whites (although often not really). People of color have never been fully included in the American dream, which now appears to be dying under the bulk of its own dysfunction.

The terms *white privilege* and *white fragility* are becoming more widespread. Both convey the problematic nature of whiteness within a country that is based on systems of oppression where white people are on top. It is interesting that some of the qualities of narcissism mirror those found within white privilege and white fragility: a grandiose sense of self, arrogance, very low empathy for others, shamelessness, hypersensitivity to critique (fragile ego), and an overall constant need to feel more special than others.

It is important to note that while whiteness and narcissism are related, narcissism is by no means restricted to white people, and in some cases, people of color exhibit higher rates of narcissism. The link here is the connection between narcissism and poverty. Consumerism continually bombards us with the need for higher status. These messages hit harder on someone who has less, as they see they are lacking according to the accepted standard. Living in a society that devalues one's identity based on skin color coupled with a devaluing of one's identity based on class can create a very fragile ego that seeks special attention.

The connections between racism and narcissism are tricky, and we will look at them more deeply in an upcoming chapter.

☧ ☧ ☧

We live in a time where the ecological crisis has escalated to such a dangerous point that human life can no longer continue its current course if we wish to live within a healthy planet. While most scientists and leaders addressing climate change are doing so on more technical and policy-based platforms, we need to look at how the views we hold and the resulting actions we take affect one another and nature. In the upcoming chapters, we will look at the narcissistic patterns within our society, how they relate to our ecological crisis, and how awakening to our more authentic selves assists in our personal and collective planetary healing.

In chapter 2, we will go deeper into narcissism in general and how it pervades our current society, as well as more clearly distinguish it from the extreme form of narcissistic personality disorder. In particular, we will look at how we became unhealthy, introducing concepts such as damaged trust, ontogenetic crippling or arrested development, and the false self. In chapter 3, we will make the connections between how our overemphasis on an egocentric self has led to the destruction of ecological and social systems. This will include more on the connection between narcissism and racism. In chapter 4, we will investigate our false self at several levels, ranging from our everyday experience to more metaphysical or spiritual concerns. I will bring in Buddhist teachings about the *skandhas*—the "aggregates" that, in Buddhism, are thought to constitute the self—and the demon of egocentricity. We will also dive into current archetypes of demons and monsters that we continually see in popular media and how these relate to narcissism. In the final chapter, we will move toward healing, diving into practices—such as attending to our emotions, practicing mindfulness, and cultivating compassion—that contribute to our individual and collective healing. By going deeply into these qualities, we will start to build our understanding of our patterns and work directly with them in a manner that supports ourselves as well as the larger web of life.

The main goal of this book is to bring awareness to the issue of narcissism, how it is affecting our common and individual welfare, how this is harming Earth, and what we can do to foster healing. *Returning the Self to Nature* does not offer a one-size-fits-all solution to our individual and collective crises, but I hope the analyses and practices here can take their place among the many options we have to address our individual and collective suffering. Throughout the book I will periodically ask you to reflect on your experiences, so you can see how your views relate to the subject matter and whether you see areas that you wish to change. I will also offer grounding practices that offer support. The first exercise is below. I hope this book sparks greater wellness for us all!

---

### EXERCISE
#### ROOTING IN SELF, ROOTING IN EARTH

In this opening exercise, I offer you a way to ground in your body, mind, and emotions when engaging this work (and in any situations you may find helpful). The content we are engaging is pretty heavy, and the intention of the book is to be able to see and change the intensity. While reading is important to awakening, we need to bring this new understanding to our practices and actions to make long-lasting changes. With this first exercise, read it through once or twice and then start the practice. I recommend coming back to this practice often as you engage with the book.

֍ ֍ ֍

Get into a comfortable seated position—whether on a chair, the floor, a cushion, or even outside. You should be relaxed but upright. Make your eyes soft, not staring at anything; or even close your eyes if this feels comfortable. Allow your body to be heavy—let your legs, sit bones (your seat), feet, and arms relax and be supported by the ground.

Imagine that you have roots forming from the base of your sit bones that plunge deep into the earth—through the carpet or floor below, through any story levels, through the cement—eventually finding rich earth. Let your roots expand widely, feeling the sustenance of Earth. Allow your belly to be soft, and begin breathing deeply from your belly, generating heat. Let your inhales and exhales be deep, taking in cleansing air. Notice your posture and let your torso be upright. Elongate your neck and slightly tuck your chin.

Relax your mouth and jaw—you might even want to stretch out your mouth and stick out your tongue for a moment. Relax your face. Relax your eyes once more. Imagine the crown of your head has long branches reaching toward the sky that mirror your roots below. Notice any areas of pain or discomfort in your body and send a deep breath to those spaces.

Touch into your heart and notice if there is a dominant emotion that arises. Silently name and honor this emotion, acknowledging that this is just one of many lenses through which you are experiencing right now. Sit in silence for a minute or two and gently come back into your surroundings.

# FRAMING NARCISSISM

One of the most precious joys I experience is being in the natural world surrounding my home. I have the privilege of living in a forested area in the foothills outside of Boulder, Colorado. While each season and moment bring change, there is a constancy and evenness of the sheltering trees, the resident birds, the rolling hills and distant mountains, and the expansive skies that often indicate what conditions are on their way. In these moments, it is easy to find a sense of centeredness, a feeling that everything is as it should be.

While humans are most certainly part of the natural world, it is often more challenging to find this sense of grounded calm in people-dominated spaces. Yet it certainly exists. We are innately constructed to access this sense of centeredness—to be in harmony with one another and ourselves. This belief forms the backdrop to my understanding that we are in the midst of a massive societal change from feeling connected to ourselves and our communities to feeling alienated from our true selves and others amid a haze of self-absorption and self-centeredness. We have become a narcissistic culture, spending so much of our time seeking the attention and approval of others. While the desire to be acknowledged and understood is completely healthy, more and more it feels like we are swimming among a sea of fools, each of us wanting to be seen and admired to a dangerously unhealthy extent.

*Do I look okay? Am I the right weight and shape? Are my hair and clothes on trend? Do I have the right job, the right car, the right home? Are people noticing me for the very special person I am? Do they like my posts? What about now? And what about now—am I still being seen?* When our self-worth is limited to the opinions of others, we are in trouble. We become consumed with how we seem to others; we become self-obsessed. *I am in love with myself. I am incredible. I hate myself. I am worthless. Oh wait, I am wonderful again:* these statements may sound ridiculous, dramatic, and even tragic, yet such narratives have come to dominate so much of our mental and social space. We have become a culture that is addicted to itself, especially in the sense of constantly curating the images we present to the outside world. Fewer and fewer of us have a stable connection to an authentic sense of self.

In this chapter, we will peer into the dynamics of our increasing collective narcissism, in part by further defining narcissism and NPD. We will examine what factors cause narcissism, what narcissism looks like, and why it is an expanding problem. Please keep in mind as you read this chapter that the literature about narcissism and NPD grows every day as more and more people encounter narcissists or become troubled by a sense of increasing narcissism in themselves. Research on narcissism is an emergent field, and while common patterns are clear, researchers of the subject do not always agree. The survey of the research that I put forth here will lay the ground for our next chapter, which establishes our individual and collective narcissism in the context of our ecological crisis.

As I disclosed in the previous chapter, I am not a therapist or clinical psychologist. I come to this topic through my work in ecopsychology, a field that examines how our disconnection from nature has resulted in the ecological crisis and our increasing mental, emotional, and physical illnesses. While ecopsychology has the word *psychology* within it, the field critiques traditional psychology for being focused on the individual person rather than being Earth and community centered. Please keep this critique in mind as we engage some of the psychological concepts that follow. Psychology itself may be narcissistic to the extent that it keeps us focused on our smaller selves rather than on the greater good.

## ORIGINS OF NARCISSISM: DAMAGED TRUST

Many of us sense that the world is off-kilter, that something is deeply wrong with our society. While the very nature of life guarantees suffering, there seems to be an increasing level of needless suffering that is cloaking much of our population in mental and physical health disorders. The compounding of such suffering has spiraled into collective trauma. So many people are fearful and anxious, experiencing the world, particularly other humans, as threatening. People seem disenchanted with and distrustful of life. But we didn't start out that way as children. Though there are of course exceptions, children in general take a curious, trusting, and even loving approach to their world. Children mirror the heart of basic goodness—that in our inherent, natural state we experience a sense of trust and care that allows us to remain open and kind. It is only through painful experience that we learn to limit or counteract those qualities.

Each of us has a first experience of disappointment with the nature of people. For some folks, this happens within their childhood household, often involving a traumatic experience with a parent or caregiver. For others, it occurs in early experiences outside of the home, such as at school, camp, a relative's home, or with a group of friends. For those fortunate to have had fairly healthy and loving childhoods, the first betrayals may take place in later schooling, in first romantic relationships, in first jobs, or even within community tragedies. It is not a comparison—my point is that inevitably in anyone's life, there will be moments of realization that other people are not always kind and caring, that people can be thoughtless and cruel. Our trust in someone is damaged, perhaps permanently, and we experience our first heartbreak and disenchantment with human nature.

I mention the universality of such experiences because it brings us to what is perhaps the most compassionate approach to understanding unhealthy narcissism and NPD: we start with what creates the early conditions for someone to become a narcissist. In chapter 1, we learned that NPD falls under the category of cluster B disorders—other such disorders include antisocial personality disorder, borderline personality disorder, and histrionic disorder. However, unlike the other three, in general, NPD is not passed down genetically. There are some conditions of temperament that come into play with narcissism, but the strongest factors are the primary care and nurturance received as a child.

We are all affected by the ways in which we were treated by our primary caregivers, typically our parents, and those suffering from narcissism and NPD are no exception. Let's approach this topic using the lens of object relations theory, a school of thought and research within contemporary psychology. In essence, object relations theory correlates the attention we received from our primary caregivers with our adult personality patterns. There are two typical "faulty" patterns: *attention withdrawn too early* and *excessive early demands*. Basically, this translates into having a parent or caregiver who either did not pay enough attention to the child or who forced the child to cater to their adult needs. In either case, the result is the child having damaged trust in people. Because a child is fundamentally dependent on the care of adults, this damaged trust often leads to their developing a false sense of self that perpetually accommodates to the needs of others. This is a strategy to receive care for oneself by taking care of others, which effects an unhealthy reversal in the child-adult energy pattern.[1]

Few of us think we received the perfect balance of attention and independence growing up. Parenting is a difficult venture indeed, and there's a lot to be said for the "good enough" parent. Yet the care of people exhibiting high levels of narcissism seems to follow the patterns of having too much attention, not enough, or a mixture of the two. In the case of too much attention, for example, there are parents who have extremely high expectations of their kids, promoting their specialness at a very early age. This sets the stage for these children to feel high levels of pressure and to fear the possibility of failure. These kids may learn to have an inflated sense of self from parents who tell them how extraordinary they are in comparison to others and how successful they will be. It is not uncommon for a child raised by a narcissistic parent to become a narcissist. The parent is already consumed by their looks, finances, and other outward forms of status to such a high degree that they care little for the emotional needs of their child, instead orienting the child to their own lenses of success. The child may receive big bursts of attention concerning their appearance and performance but little empathy and nurturance, and they must learn to focus on someone else's idea of their image rather than on their own needs.

In contrast, yet with similar results, a caregiver who gives little attention to their child can set a pattern in which the child always wants to please others, once again maintaining an outward focus rather than meeting their own needs. A parent may be too caught up in their work, other relationships, addictions, or an array of possible things. Whatever it may be that occupies the parent's attention, if the child does not feel seen and attended to, they may grow up to continually seek attention from others. In some cases, the child may experience both too much and too little attention from their primary caregivers. Perhaps one parent places excessive demands on the child, while another is cold and distant. This split approach is even possible within one parent—for instance, if they overfocus on material goods *and* underfocus on feeling and expressing emotions.

The result of attention withdrawn too early or excessive

early demands is damaged trust. A young child has the experience of their needs being unmet and therefore suffers an underdeveloped sense of self. The environmental psychologists Deborah Du Nann Winter and Susan M. Koger claim that narcissism is one of four possible "neurotic conditions" that result from this damaged trust, along with "depression, paranoia, and compulsion."[2] As we will see, someone exhibiting narcissism may exhibit all these traits. Having this sense of damaged trust creates a perpetual feeling of unsafety in the world and an inhibited sense of self. It creates the conditions for the child to grow into a hurt and distrustful person who is not centered in an authentic understanding of their own identity and needs. Moreover, it creates the conditions for the child to have an overwhelming need for attention as they equate receiving attention with worthiness and lovability, which is incredibly sad.

An important role of the parent is to *mirror* the child in a way that lets them know they are seen and loved while also providing feedback. Everyone has a need to be mirrored by those they are in relationship with—to be understood and praised for the type of person they are and for the things that they do. If you have ever been in a relationship with someone who pays little attention to who you are and instead focuses on you meeting *their* needs, you probably have a good understanding of what it feels like not to be seen and cared about in a genuine way. Perhaps you even had this experience as a child.

## THE FALSE SELF

In general, people who are narcissistic or who may even have developed NPD had damaging experiences in their early childhoods where they were not given appropriate attention—not given the empathy, nurturance, and love they so needed. A child who does not receive healthy mirroring may absorb the notion that people will not see them for the distinct person they are and will not demonstrate care and love for them. The child misses out on receiving helpful guidance—both positive and corrective—on their behaviors. This can result in a child, and later an adult, who is emotionally reckless, neither able to contain their emotions nor take responsibility for them. Instead they project their negative emotions onto others in disruptive ways.

Another way of describing this process is the development of a *false self*—an identity that separates from the signals received from others and instead creates a reality where they are the most important person. In chapter 4, we will go more deeply into the term *false self*, especially to explore how it is understood differently in ecopsychology as compared to traditional psychology. The concept of the false self was first coined by the psychoanalyst Donald Winnicott and has been employed within the fields of psychology and human development to examine ego expression and repression, most prominently within the context of narcissism.[3] For our purposes in unpacking narcissism, we can simply understand that the *false self* serves to protect the child from neglectful care, creating a sort of fantasy world where they are the central actor.

For a narcissist, the *false self* was constructed to create a bounded world where they can no longer be hurt by excessive demands, criticisms, and lack of love from others. In the reality of the false self, the narcissist simply does not acknowledge these painful experiences as real. Instead, the narcissist inhabits a new reality in which everything revolves around them—they are the star of the show and the center of the universe. And just as others did not give them the care, attention, and love they needed, they have little capacity to give these qualities to others. The fictitious reality of the narcissist only lets in good input, rejecting experiences that make them feel bad. A narcissist lacks what psychologists refer to as *object constancy*—the ability to allow people and experiences to be a mixture of both good and bad qualities.[4] The narcissist shuns people they see as bad, removing them—permanently, if possible—from their experience.

Since the narcissist has created a false reality, they do not recognize that they are emotionally immature. A narcissist thus displays arrested development. Their maturity level has not progressed past the stage of early childhood or at most the teenage years, and so their behavior is quite juvenile and manipulative when they do not receive the attention or outcome they want. The damaged trust the narcissist developed as a child results in feeling deeply insecure. This seems ironic to those of us who have been in a close relationship with a narcissist, as they often appear overconfident and excessively prideful. This is only a mask meant to cover up their deep sense of insecurity. Narcissists not only fear that others will not love them but also have trouble loving themselves.

My emphasis so far has been on explaining how the seeds of narcissism can be planted in children through inadequate early care and nurturance. That said, some psychologists claim there is something in the narcissist's biological makeup that contributes to their condition. While these studies are interesting and relevant, at this point they remain inconclusive. It may be likely that narcissism has a biological component, yet we do not know this for certain. What we do know is that the early childhood of the narcissist sets the stage for their behavior.

## THE STORY OF NARCISSUS

I have really good relationships with my parents. They have been married for well over half a century, and I feel so fortunate that both are alive and an important part of my life. My father is quite a character. He is truly self-made—an African American man who grew up in a tough neighborhood in Harlem, on welfare, going to city college, starting in the mail room of his industry, and eventually becoming a leader in television advertising. It would be an understatement to say he is both charming and funny. During my childhood, most nights during dinner, he would come home with new stories and jokes. He always looked great, wearing stylish suits and leisure wear, and he always worked out to stay in shape. He is retired now, but he still takes great care of himself. For decades, one of my favorite gotcha rituals my father would perform would go something like this.

Dad: I can't wait until tomorrow!
Me: Why?
Dad: Because I getter better looking every day!

This bad dad joke, which always produced a smile on both of our faces, actually comes from the famous football star Joe Namath, and it was even the title of a book that came out before I was born.[5] Yet to me, this was my dad's signature saying. Coming from him, it conveyed an affable sense of confidence and positivity, yet there is something about it that reminds me of narcissism. Now, as I said in chapter 1, we are all somewhere on the narcissism spectrum, and my dad definitely tilts to the higher side. (Sorry, Dad.) But this is an example of healthy narcissism, where someone displays high self-esteem and, at the same time, can move beyond their ego and focus on the greater good.

Even so, this image of my dad—perhaps in part because he often said those lines while standing in front of a mirror—reminds me of the classic depiction of Narcissus, the character from Greek mythology for whom narcissism is named. There are many versions of the myth: In short, Narcissus is a young man, a hunter, birthed from a union between a river god and a nymph. He is incredibly beautiful, and his parents worry that his attractiveness will hinder him by making him arrogant and overly focused on his looks. In some versions of the myth, Narcissus spurns a young man who loves him, while in another the wounded feelings belong to Echo, a woodland nymph who fell in love with him. In all versions Narcissus is cursed, which results in him seeing and falling in love with his reflection. He does not recognize the image as his own reflection and, unable to get the love he desires, ends up killing himself. The myth, which has inspired many works of art, has developed an archetypal place in modern psychology through its analysis by the early twentieth-century psychologists Sigmund Freud and Carl Jung, as well as others. It is a grim story, indeed, and a parody on the tragedy of self-consumption.

On a side note, I am fascinated with Echo's role in this

myth. She is a nymph who has been cursed by the goddess Hera and so can only repeat the last words that she hears. When she meets Narcissus and falls madly in love with him, she is unable to intelligibly communicate with him, so he shuns her. Narcissism and NPD often come up in pop culture in story lines where someone has been deeply hurt by a narcissist. While in the myth Narcissus does not become obsessed with his reflection until after his encounter with Echo, I see a metaphor wherein the narcissistic victim is like Echo. Like her, they are trapped in a world where they are unable to be truly recognized for themselves and where the person they love is self-consumed, unable to love or empathize with them, leaving the victim an "echo" of themselves.

Considering our focus on ecopsychology—developed more in our next chapter—there is an irony within the story of Narcissus. He is cursed to fall in love with his image, which is classically illustrated as staring at his reflection in a body of water. How many countless hours did he spend looking at his reflection without ever seeing the precious water? This is metaphoric of the disconnection between humans and nature and our resulting illness. If only Narcissus had looked past his image and seen the water: deep, cool, both moving and still, mysterious, transparent, and reflective of the beauty of nature—of sun, trees, clouds, birds, and stars. Perhaps the guidance of water would have knocked Narcissus to his senses!

## THE NARCISSISTIC MONSTER:
## AN INDIVIDUALIZED ARCHETYPE

Having considered the issue of damaged trust and its role in childhood development, you may be wondering why narcissists are often portrayed in such negative light—as monsters, demons, vampires, evildoers. After all, it seems clear that they are merely adults who were molded by insufficient childhoods. Perhaps the reason for the demonization is the sheer intensity of the experience of being in relationship with an extreme narcissist. If you have ever been in a close relationship with someone with NPD, you know they can be maddening and severely damaging to your self-esteem and well-being. I can recall some of the worst moments I had with my ex where he would become volatile when I talked on the phone to a male friend or even a family member; he would verbally attack me, accusing me of trying to make him jealous. He would also suddenly have an emergency right as we were leaving to meet my friends or loved ones, causing us to cancel or be rudely late. My ex became so possessive that he would insist I leave my car at his place and that we share his car all the time, so I was constantly attached to him. My world kept getting smaller and smaller, and more centered on his. In extreme cases, a narcissist can destroy your finances, your relationships with others, your mental health, and even your life. So let's dive deeper into what narcissism and NPD entail to better understand the role that narcissism plays in our society.

The research literature on narcissism is vast and constantly expanding. There are some excellent, in-depth books on this subject—many of which I list in the resources toward the end of the book. Although we will not get into every little detail about narcissism and NPD here, we will explore the topic enough to provide a foundation for the connection between narcissism and our collective crises.

In chapter 1, we learned that everyone displays levels of narcissism, and that a certain amount of this self-centeredness is healthy. It is only when people exhibit very high levels of narcissism that it becomes problematic. We also learned that people with NPD are characterized by more extreme traits compared to nonclinical narcissists. These traits include a grandiose sense of self, arrogance, very low empathy for others, shamelessness, hypersensitivity to critique (fragile ego), and an overall constant need to feel more special than others. Now we'll take a closer look at these common traits and then move into some of the unique forms of narcissism. In general, within this section I will use the terms *narcissism* and *NPD* interchangeably, referring to people with extreme narcissism regardless of whether they have been diagnosed with NPD.

## Arrogance and Grandiose Sense of Self

We have seen that people with high levels of narcissism typically had difficulties with their primary care as young children. Due to this, they create their own worlds in an effort to feel safe, central, and more important than others. They identify their character as being superior to most people, overestimate their abilities, and perceive themselves to be highly successful, skillful, and attractive—perhaps even perfect. This superiority complex or grandiose sense of self causes people with NPD to only see their positive aspects; they are unable to see their negative qualities or to grasp the impact of their detrimental behaviors. In essence, they can do no wrong. This overblown sense of ego manifests in arrogance, where the narcissist is excessively boastful about their accomplishments and traits. While it can be wonderful to share one's achievements and positive characteristics, someone with NPD will continually self-promote with an assertiveness that lacks humility and leaves no room for others to share about their own successes.

## Lack of Empathy

While they desire and often demand a high level of attention, a narcissist has very little capacity to listen to and attend to the needs of others. This is a key flag indicating that you may be dealing with a narcissist: you share your feelings, experiences, and other aspects of yourself with them, only to be startled by a reaction of irritation or their compulsive need to redirect the conversation back to them. If you hold a higher status than a narcissist, they might feign interest in your feelings to get something they want. In general, however, narcissists have very low empathy. Many of the traits we desire in relationships—caring, compassion, trust, reciprocity, and understanding—are unlikely to come from someone with strong narcissistic tendencies. Since the narcissist, in attempting to adapt to difficult childhood conditions, long ago created a fictional reality that centers around themselves, they are unable to step into the reality of others in a sincere, loving manner.

## Shamelessness, Fragile Ego, and Hypersensitivity to Critique

Similarly, since narcissists have limited or no capacity to identify with their negative behaviors, they are often described as having very low or even no ability to feel shame. At the same time, they often experience grandiosity, which results in someone who thinks very highly of themselves, truly feels they are always right, and often resorts to shaming others in order to diminish another person's status and elevate their own.[6]

While having little shame is a trait associated with narcissism, this can be a confusing quality for researchers, because, deep down inside, narcissists do feel shame and are expending an enormous amount of energy to mask it. It is important to note that some experts claim the narcissist, with their fragile ego, has very low self-esteem, while others contend that the narcissist actually has high self-esteem. My view is that while many narcissists seem to hold high self-esteem, they are typically overcompensating to hide a deep-seated fragile ego.[7] This core vulnerability makes the narcissist unable to handle feedback, so they exhibit an extreme hypersensitivity to critique. It is not uncommon for a narcissist to become enraged when they are critiqued. They experience critique as an attack on the fictional character they have unconsciously created and believe to be their self. In fact, when a narcissist is critiqued by someone in a marked manner, it is not uncommon for the narcissist to be unable to let their comment go and they cut the person out of their life.

### Constant Need to Feel Special

Finally, a narcissist believes they are incredibly special and that, since they obviously stand out above others, the people around them should recognize this. I believe that everyone is special and unique, but a narcissist has an overall constant need to feel more special than others. It is as if they expect to be treated as if it is their birthday—showered with attention, entitled to the best options—every day. For a narcissist, the world should revolve around them.

At this point, you may be wondering why people become involved with narcissists. Why on earth would someone befriend or even fall in love with a person who is self-centered, combative, entitled, arrogant, and unable to care about others? Ironically, most narcissists are magnetizing—they often project an attractiveness and confidence that draw people in. They have spent their lives curating a false self and, at the surface level, this projection seems authentic. This charismatic facade wears thin over time, as the less appealing aspects of the narcissist come out.

❦ ❦ ❦

We have now gone over some of the most common traits of narcissists. But narcissism gets more complex, as there are many variations. This territory gets a bit confusing, as various authors, psychologists, and camps of psychology define these variations differently. We will not plunge very deeply into this topic, as we will be shifting our focus to collective narcissism, but it is worth mentioning some of these variations briefly.

The simplest and most common classification of narcissism divides it into two types—the *grandiose (overt) narcissist* and the *vulnerable (covert) narcissist*. The grandiose or overt narcissist exhibits the traits we have already covered in our previous sections, embodying the classic form of narcissism, and is the type most commonly presented in mainstream media. This is the self-centered, arrogant bully who is loud, attention hogging, and potentially dangerous. The vulnerable or covert narcissist, a less recognized type, still embodies the common traits, but they do so in a different package. Instead of aggressively thrusting themselves into the spotlight, the vulnerable narcissist comes across as needy, shy, resentful, and even depressed. They often feel that the world has missed their specialness and so they have retreated. Some narcissists are a combination of the grandiose and vulnerable characteristics, exhibiting grandiosity in certain circumstances and periods of their life and neediness in others.

As the research gets even more detailed, there are further classifications beyond these two. The clinical psychologist and professor Dr. Ramani Durvasula depicts the additional categories of the *communal narcissist*, *benign narcissist*, and *malignant narcissist*. In short, the communal narcissist appears on the surface as someone who is doing good for the world, such as taking on an important cause, yet underneath is driven by the attention they receive for their work.[8] The benign narcissist is just that—a person who is profoundly self-involved yet not very harmful to others. Both the communal and benign narcissists do not generate much attention within the literature about narcissism. The malignant narcissist is the most extreme form of narcissism. These are the narcissists who cause destruction to others and are often confused with psychopaths. It is actually not uncommon for a psychopath to be a narcissist. Psychopaths, however, are more extreme and dangerous (often having a history of illegal activities, including violence), show little to no remorse, and may assume different personalities to reach their aims. Malignant narcissists represent a very scary form of narcissism—the stalker, the manipulator, the aggressor, the liar, the cheater, the power monger. Getting involved with such a ruthless individual can be perilous, and its seriousness should not be downplayed. Mainstream culture often sensationalizes this form of narcissism through the news, talks shows, blogs, and made-for-television movies. Looking at this phenomenon can be fascinating, in part because the behavior of malignant narcissists is so unbelievable, yet also because such individuals serve as emblems of something that is growing in our society—our collective narcissism.

## FROM INDIVIDUAL TO COLLECTIVE NARCISSISM: A CULTURAL SHIFT

The world of the narcissist is not a kind space. Very few people enjoy being around someone who is self-centered, arrogant, volatile, and insincere—probably not even the narcissist. Experts recommend that a person who is in a troubling relationship with an extreme narcissist cease contact, if possible, because people with NPD rarely change. Counselors typically encourage those who have been abused by narcissists to try to sever ties, process the experience as best they can, and move on—though this can be quite difficult, especially if the narcissist is a family member or spouse. However, even if the person is successful in never having to deal with the narcissist again, the narcissist will find another person or even multiple people to receive attention from—and then the whole cycle begins again.

But what if it isn't an isolated narcissist we are trying to avoid? What if, as discussed above, our entire society is becoming narcissistic? Now our understanding of the problem has to develop away from something damaging yet discrete, like a car accident, and toward something slower, steadier, and even more insidious—the enculturation of toxicity, like the breathing of polluted air. In my view, this is exactly what is happening in our world today, and it's been building for a long time. Western societies—and, arguably, any society that is heavily influenced by a Western-dominated, materialistic worldview—are swimming in narcissism.

Think of the classical illustration of Narcissus, staring at himself in a pond. Today we are surrounded by people who are self-consumed with their own image, and we are regularly prompted to enter that state ourselves. Think about social media platforms where folks ceaselessly post about themselves—the relentless selfies; the constant need to look good to the outward world, even when things are not great. More and more, our culture encourages us to focus solely on ourselves—it is becoming pathological. We have a need to be someone special and, to a certain extent, this is not surprising. In the United States, we live in a country that is hyperindividualized. Essentially, the rights of the privatized individual are held as the golden mean and come with the expectation of competition to be at the top. Think of common sayings such as "Look out for number one" or "It is every man for himself." The "American dream" tells us that we must struggle in the fight to get to the top, and if we work hard enough, we will get there. Yet where there is a top, there is a bottom. The Darwinian concept of "survival of the fittest" is taken to a new level, where we often feel that the world is a hostile place, and unless we compete against others and win, we will fall to the bottom and essentially lose.

It comes as no surprise, then, that for many, we live in a mean world. The term for this, *mean world syndrome*, was coined by the communications researcher George Gerbner, who studied the influence of violence in the media on the general population. In short, his research revealed that while the increase of violence exhibited on television and in other forms of media did not increase the amount of violence in the world, it did increase people's perception of the world as a violent, mean place.[9] The more people consume media violence, the more violent the world appears. This finding causes me to wonder about the effects of the ever-proliferating media content by and about narcissistic people. Does mean world syndrome have a parallel that we might call *narcissistic world syndrome*? The influences supporting a me-centered worldview go beyond our social media posts; they include the ads that bombard us with messages about the goods and services we need to be our best selves, as well as the images we constantly see that describe the successful person—fit, good-looking, wealthy, independent, self-made. This is not a self that strives to help others but one concerned with self-interest. We are so surrounded by selfishness that it often appears as the new normal.

So many of our current stories reinforce this mean and me-centered world. Reality television shows highlight characters who are ruthless and self-centered. There are endless depictions of evil villains, vampires, zombies, serial killers, and other psychopaths in movies, television, podcasts, comics, and books. People seem to eat up these themes that reinforce a view of a world divided by good and evil, self and other. And then the actual news perpetually illustrates all the perils that pervade our society—murders, corruption, violence, terrorism, poverty, ecological disasters, racism, misogyny. Many of the perpetrators of our time—whether real or fictitious; whether a monster, a reality television star, a politician, or a corporation—appear as self-centered, manipulative, and highly dangerous, demonstrating that the world is not a safe place. It is no wonder that the world appears hostile.

❧ ❧ ❧

In his late-1970s groundbreaking book *The Culture of Narcissism*, the cultural critic Christopher Lasch forewarned about our growing collective narcissism.

> Americans have retreated to purely personal preoccupations. Having no hope of improving their lives in any of the ways that matter, people have convinced themselves that what matters is psychic self-improvement: getting in touch with their feelings, eating health food, taking lessons in ballet or belly dancing, immersing themselves in the wisdom of the East, jogging, learning how to "relate," overcoming the "fear of pleasure." Harmless in themselves, these pursuits, elevated to a program and wrapped in the rhetoric of authenticity and awareness, signify a retreat from politics and a repudiation of the recent past.[10]

He used the label *the new narcissist* to describe a trend toward self-centeredness within what he saw as the closing era of unbridled capitalism.

Lasch identified one component of the new narcissism as the spread of materialism from products to people themselves as they sought, and were encouraged to seek, physical and psychic well-being to soothe their despair and apathy about the lack of meaningful social or political change. Traditional capitalism focused on the production of material goods. While this kind of production remains important, the offshoring of manufacturing plants and jobs has led to a major shift in Western capitalism. Now the consumption of services that revolve around the individual has taken center stage. While past generations might have gone to the barber, the doctor, and a few other service providers, it is not uncommon for today's adults to go to the hairdresser, massage therapist, yoga teacher, personal trainer, life coach, sleep doctor, acupuncturist, nutritionist, and psychotherapist. Okay, I know that list sounds dramatic and expensive, but you get the point. Lasch saw this kind of materialistic self-centeredness as one aspect of the new narcissism. He coupled it with the effects of postmodernity, wherein so many people no longer hold a common viewpoint. The loss of shared culture marks a shift away from any commonly held truth, such that the individual is "free" to author their own unique reality. The new narcissists Lasch described are tragically liberated. Although they assert their independence and self-investment, they remain enmeshed in an anxiety-ridden, capitalistic worldview through which everyone appears as a potential competitor.

Reflecting on Lasch's contentions about the new narcissist, I resonate greatly with his pinpointing the excessive focus on self-development we currently see in our society. At the same time, I feel that cultivating a focus on personal healing is important. The key is having balance and awareness. A society that focuses on self-care to such an extent that it ignores greater political, economic, and social realities of the world is dangerous. If folks are able to work with larger issues and their personal wellness, however, the possibilities for radical societal transformation abound. The term *community care* has arisen within social justice communities—particularly groups of women of color—to describe this possibility. The term is based on the writer and activist Audre Lorde's statement, "Caring for myself is not self-indulgence, it is self-preservation, and that is an act of political warfare."[11] This view of self-care is in sharp contrast to what Lasch saw within the new narcissism, and it holds great potential. Masses of people, particularly those within so-called marginalized positionalities, are actively dedicating their lives to global issues such as racism, poverty, identity politics, and the environment. They realize that to do this work, they need to focus on not only their personal wellness but that of their communities of solidarity. When self-development includes the wellness of the whole, the danger of the new narcissism is quelled.

❀ ❀ ❀

If we briefly revisit the common developmental structure of individual narcissism in the context of our emerging collective narcissism, a clearer picture starts to form. In the case of the individual narcissist, we typically find that a primary caregiver did not foster a strong sense of self and security in the child. Over time, the child adapted to this situation by forming a false self whose reality, while badly out of touch, ensured a kind of pseudo-independence and stabilized a certain delusion of safety, and the child carried forward these habits into adulthood. For collective narcissism, in place of parents or caregivers, we have a consumer culture based on perpetual desire that fosters insecure false selves on a mass scale. As with parenting, this begins in childhood; unlike parenting, it does not come to a close: we absorb this culture throughout our lives. Advertisements and other forms of media monopolize our understanding of self, focusing us outward on superficial yet unattainable ideals. Such ideals promote homogeneity of vision while telling us that we are supposed to be uniquely special and if we try hard enough, we can be. As is evident in the life stories of many millionaires and billionaires, the consumer hamster wheel has no stopping point; there is always another level of wealth, power, influence, or conspicuous consumption to achieve—a bigger yacht, a more powerful lobbying group, a first private trip to space. What kind of basis for sane selfhood is that?

In this cultural context, the modern individual is encouraged to author their own tale of specialness, essentially creating their own reality in which they must look the best, get the highest grades, buy the most expensive things, and have the most impressive job. The "most," "best," and "highest" are necessarily in comparison to others, causing unneeded competition against our friends, neighbors, coworkers, classmates, and family members. Our need to be *better than* causes us to be overly prideful, arrogant, and boastful about our accomplishments, with little awareness of how this affects others and ourselves. When we do not meet these ideal standards, we become vulnerable, defensive, depressed, and dissatisfied, damaging our already fragile egos. We perpetuate cycles of creating the persona of who we want to be, aggressively projecting this image to the world, and crashing when our expectations are not realized.

As will be clear by now, our culture of narcissism is closely associated with consumerism. The combination of media, fierce individualism, and capitalism in Western societies, paired with this new self-consumption, results in excessive spending to prop up our false images of ourselves. This can result in economic disaster on both personal and collective scales. In "The All-Consuming Self," their essay from the mid-1990s, Kanner and Gomes laid out the patterns of consumerism that are tied to narcissism and this false image in US culture.[12] Our excessive sense of entitlement paired with feelings of emptiness is linked to spending extremes that lead to massive debt and further levels of anxiety and low self-esteem.[13] The capitalistic nature of our society reinforces this trend because as more people soothe their low self-esteem and privilege with more spending, corporate earnings skyrocket. It is profitable to keep us self-absorbed and insecure. Linking this to Lasch's analysis of the new narcissist, the various services we employ to promote our self-worth—from health care to physical fitness and even therapy—are also often profit-oriented.

Let us look at two more traits associated with individual narcissism that can help us further unpack narcissism on the collective level. The first is *gaslighting*. This term, which has come into much more common use in recent years, means the act of denying someone else's experience of reality by subtly or forcefully contradicting the validity of their perceptions, emotions, thoughts, or behaviors. If you have ever been on the receiving end of a narcissist's gaslighting, you probably felt perplexed, even shocked, and hurt. The narcissist employs gaslighting as a tactic to wound their victims: "How dare you say that my being late is selfish? I don't even know why I come when you always act like this. *You're the one* who is selfish." Basically the narcissist denies reality and replaces it with a false reality, causing the other person to question their sanity and feel unstable. The narcissist displaces a world in which they may be the wrongdoer with an alternate reality in which they are in the right and someone else, usually the victim, is in error. In sum, it is a form of psychological and emotional abuse.[14]

When we apply the concept of gaslighting to collective narcissism, we may recognize it in the cognitive dissonance many of us experience in relation to a self-centered materialistic culture. At heart, we are well aware that the meaning of life has little to do with how much money we have, what we look like, and what status we hold, yet we allow ourselves to fall into the trap of chasing after these things and judging ourselves by false standards. Those of us who have chosen to focus on different goals may encounter negative feedback from the larger society and even from those close to us, suggesting that we are chasing illusions—hiding from the real world. A great example of this is how many female-identified people of color are embracing their bodies, beauty, intelligence, and power within a society that tells people that being thin, white, blond, and silent is the standard. Today we see more and more folks disrupting these norms and showcasing their full bodies and voices with zeal.

The second term worth mentioning is *schadenfreude*.[15] This German word denotes unkindness of a particular variety. Schadenfreude occurs when someone delights in another person's downfall. A narcissist practices schadenfreude because they perceive others' failures as status increases for themselves. To take pleasure in the suffering of another being, even your perceived enemy, is cruel. However, in our narcissistic world, this is not uncommon. Much of the draw to narcissistic personae, such as those of the reality star or the bare-knuckle politician, is the entertainment people receive from seeing them treat others cruelly. It reaffirms the "it's a dog-eat-dog world" mentality, where we must compete against one another to obtain success. It reinforces the need to look out for number one, because no one else will look out for you.

Some Jungian psychologists see our collective narcissism as an archetype that is overtaking our culture. Archetypes are the stories, myths, art, and symbols we use to represent ourselves. They are not always blatantly manifest, often remaining hidden in our collective unconscious. We are always living within a cultural story that is embodied within an archetype. The "American dream" is an archetype where the hardworking individual can climb the ladder of success. The current obsession with superheroes is another archetype where good always prevails over evil and someone with special powers will save the day. While often helpful, archetypes are not necessarily true. They are stories we would like to believe, similar to myths or origin stories. Alluding to narcissism, the physician and Jungian psychologist Dr. Steven Buser notes that a collective archetype may form in response to "complexes that provoke unusual mass behavior."[16] Could it be possible that the growth of narcissism in individuals is laying the ground for our collective story, whether consciously or unconsciously?

A society based on narcissism leaves individuals little time to focus outward on other people and little to no time to focus on outward issues. *If I am consumed with the preparation, execution, and maintenance of my image, how can I help a loved one? If I barely have time for my loved ones, how can I serve my community?*

*If I do not have time for my community, how can I serve Earth?* In our next chapter, we will engage these questions, looking at the ways in which our collective narcissism is divorced from its relationship to and responsibilities toward Earth. This investigation will take us deeply into an ecopsychological view of narcissism.

---

## EXERCISE
### SHAKING OUR BRANCHES

If you have made it to the end of the chapter, you may be feeling somewhat agitated and overwhelmed. I find that going deeply into the topics of individual and collective narcissism can lead me to feel as if I have been cloaked in a heavy film of dread. In chapter 1, we ended with an exercise to get us grounded in our bodies, breath, and the earth. I truly do encourage you to revisit that first exercise as often as is helpful.

Here I offer a second exercise to help you shake off a bit of the heavy feelings that may be lingering for you. This exercise builds from the first. I highly encourage you to try it—sometimes we don't realize how a seemingly simple practice can transform our experience. You are also welcome to come back to this exercise anytime it may be helpful.

❀ ❀ ❀

Find a quiet place away from other people. This can be indoors or outside—wherever you feel most comfortable and have space to move your body.

Once you are in your spot, stretch out your body a little. Stretch your arms over your head. Take a deep yawn, stretching out your mouth; stick out your tongue, and remember to relax your jaw. Roll your shoulders forward and then back. Bend your torso a bit, allowing your butt to stick out; put your hands on your hips and bend forward a little bit and then bend back slightly. Move your hips, shake out your legs, and wiggle your toes and fingers.

Once you have stretched your body a bit, find a comfortable standing position with your feet firmly planted on the ground and your body upright and tall. Begin taking deep breaths that start from your belly and come up to your crown.

Close your eyes. Imagine you have roots that sprout from your feet and burrow deep into the ground below you. Imagine the crown of your head has long branches reaching toward the sky that mirror your roots below. Imagine that you are a beautiful fall tree covered with brilliantly colored leaves. Maybe they are red, or yellow, or perhaps orange. In fact, in this visualization, you could be covered in many brilliant colors. Imagine your arms multiplied into many branches that are covered in leaves that are ready to fall.

As you visualize the branches of your crown and arms, let each leaf shimmer in the light of the sun. While each leaf is an aspect of you, this is not all of you, just a temporary part of you. Allow these leaves to represent your conditionings. Honoring the uniqueness and beauty of each leaf, begin to shake your arms and gently roll your head. As you do this, see these beautiful leaves fall away.

Keep moving until all your leaves have fallen. When your branches are completely bare, come back to your breath and stand firmly in your feet and body—your roots and trunk. Notice what it feels like to be in this moment. When you are ready, slowly open your eyes and come back to your surroundings.

# 3

---

# ECOLOGICAL CRISIS
# AND NARCISSISTIC
# PERSONALITY DISORDER

The stories we repeatedly tell our children and ourselves are the stories that take hold in our psyches and concretize our reality. These stories, along with other symbolism, art, and myths, help form the collective archetypes that capture the essence of our society. The word *ontology* is used to describe the belief systems we employ—our origin stories, our worldviews. A worldview comprises two primary dimensions—habits of mind and resulting points of view. The habits of mind are the things we inherit, the ideas we are conditioned to believe. These include our religion, gender identity, political views, and systems of morality. Our resulting points of view are the ways we act out our habits of mind— the choices and actions we make based on how we have been conditioned to think about ourselves and the world.[1] While most of us like to think we hold unique identities and points of view, the conditioning we receive from our overarching culture is paramount. Many of us are not conscious of these dominating stories and this conditioning, yet we are still acting them out.

There is a stark difference between many of the myths or origin stories within earth-based, Indigenous cultures and those of Western civilizations. Indigenous cultures around the world align with what are often termed *the original instructions*—sacred teachings from the spirit world, ancestors, and elders that focus on how humans must live in right relationship with all of life. At the core of these teachings is respect and reciprocity—the belief that everything is sacred and must be treated as such. Rivers, mountains, trees, and animals are often seen as elders with deep wisdom, and Earth is viewed as a sacred world. These views are also held by many wisdom lineages within Buddhism, Paganism, and other traditions, both nonsecular and secular, that predate Western societies. We should not romanticize these traditions' teachings as portraying everything to be all one and joyful. All beings have various qualities that can invoke fear, anger, joy, delight, and so forth. The stories told by these traditions mirror this multiplicity yet their emphasis is on reciprocation and being in right relationship.

In contrast, many of the central stories of Western culture overemphasize evil within the world and hence the need to be fearful. Our stories separate the human world from the natural world and position humans as having dominion over and being more important than other beings. Within this chapter, we will look at how our society's collective separation from the natural world has resulted in a culture that is divorced from healthy connections with our home, Earth. We will explore how this separation has led to our growing narcissism, and we will make connections between our overemphasis on an egocentric self and the destruction of ecological and social systems. I will employ many of the lenses of ecopsychology to guide us. This topic can feel extremely intense, as it relates to each of us on an intimate personal level *and* to all of us on a very real and imminent level. As you move through this chapter, I encourage you to focus on your breath and what you are feeling in your body, and to take breaks as needed. Remember to go back to the exercises at the conclusion of chapters 1 and 2 and to spend time outside.

As noted in chapter 1, the field of ecopsychology makes four major assumptions: the planet is calling for healing; people are calling for healing; these two phenomena intertwine; and the illness is embedded within the history and present of Western civilization. Fundamentally, ecopsychology looks at the disconnection humans of Western civilization (and by extension anyone living under systems of corporate globalization) have from the rest of nature. While it has the word *psychology* within it, ecopsychology as a discipline formed in part to critique mainstream psychology, as the latter often seeks to help people fit into a status quo that ecopsychology sees as damaging. By contrast, ecopsychologists respond to both the human and ecological crises by explicitly identifying that our separation from nature is causing severe harm to ourselves and to the planet. The field voices a deep recognition of our brokenness as well as of the destruction we are causing to Earth. A few ecopsychologists address narcissism in minor ways, and many address the collective trauma most of us experienced in our early childhoods, but this book is the first sustained attempt to see narcissism through the lens of ecopsychology. Within this chapter we will look again at the patterns of narcissism, this time framing the topic within the larger patterns of our ecological and social crises.

## SEPARATION: OUR NATURE-HUMAN SPLIT

Often when I am teaching or doing a public talk, I like to remind my audience that we are animals. It is a silly, rudimentary thing to say, as we all know that we are mammals, which are animals. Yet our society paints us as something quite different, so I think we can use the reminder more often.

We are animals dependent upon Earth's resources for food, water, air, and ground; for sunlight and rain; for our sentience—for everything that provides us life. Without Earth, we are nothing—no form, no identity, no footprint. Many Indigenous traditions, having sustained a deep sense of kinship with Earth, have gratitude practices that honor all beings. A beautiful example of this is the "Thanksgiving Address" from the Haudenosaunee peoples (the Iroquois Nation). Not to be confused with the United States' colonialist tradition of Thanksgiving, this practice is for openings and closings of gatherings and is an extremely lengthy thanking of the many animal species, plants, and other living entities of the land. It is a reminder that while humans are special, we are only one of many sacred special beings alive. Being in right relationship with the land and all beings is an important practice for earth-based communities. It is not a metaphor but rather a literal responsibility to one another and to all of life—we are in a family with all the beings of Earth.

❦   ❦   ❦

Reflecting on the beauty and harmony with which Indigenous peoples exist and treat Earth leads naturally to the question, why did humans of Western societies and then other globalized corporate civilizations break their intrinsic ties with nature? At some point, we broke away from our earth-based traditions and entered into a reality where humans were no longer one of many kinds of unique living beings within Earth and instead viewed ourselves as the most important species. This sense of specialness mirrors the sense of specialness and entitlement exhibited by narcissists. The reasons for this shift are many and complex, and the subject of many books. Though this is not the place to undertake a detailed history of this cultural transition, I want to highlight a couple of its aspects that I see as particularly important.

Some scholars claim our move away from earth-based ancestry was first prompted by fear for our survival and the need to accumulate in order to feel safe. One of my favorite authors, the psychotherapist Chellis Glendinning, calls our rift with the natural world the "original trauma."[2] Importantly, this term names that breaking away from earth-based, original traditions as having been traumatic for both humanity and Earth. Glendinning claims the primary cause of this break was the process of domestication:

No one fully understands why people began to control and manage the natural world by cultivating wild plants and taming wild animals. The most popular theory is a geo-anthropological one, positing that global climatic change some ten thousand years ago altered growing patterns all over the world and

forced people to improvise more consciously managed
livelihoods. Another school of thought suggests
that people became sedentary first, and that fenced
planting and animal husbandry naturally followed
suit. A third proposes a radical increase in population,
demanding this development of radically increased
food sources. A fourth theory points to the hunter-
gatherer practice of "budding off" to start new bands,
resulting ultimately in the impingement of one group
upon another.[3]

Therein we abandoned our thousands of years of hunter-
gatherer traditions and started living sedentary lifestyles,
amassing food through large-scale agriculture. Although
this transition took place across centuries and was somewhat
different depending on location, overall it resulted in a number of important patterned changes. These included a shift in
gender roles, with men now assuming control of hunting and
agriculture, while women were relegated to duties associated
with the home, such as raising children and preparing meals.
By living a sedentary lifestyle, women also began to have more
babies, resulting in unprecedented population growth.

Even more dramatic was the power humans now had over
nature. No longer being as dependent on the available food
sources in wild nature lessened our need to pay such close
attention to the delicate balance of the natural world. This
shift away from nature minimized our connection to its
forces and progressed to affect a vast variety of cultural and
material phenomena.

With an increasing number of people, the need for more

and more land and other resources grew, such that eventually certain groups began to attempt the colonization of other people's lands and cultures. The tools used by humans developed more sophistication and deadliness, with warfare and conquest becoming the norm. The introduction of mechanistic science further silenced the natural world, as other beings were increasingly viewed as not truly alive (this even spread to the belief that women and peoples of color were less sentient and intelligent). Seen from this lens, the world quickly became a series of independent parts as opposed to an interconnected whole.

The invention of the written word, and the attendant development of abstract thinking, is another phenomenon that had a major role in disconnecting us from nature. In general, oral cultures tend to embody and parallel nature, while cultures that developed written scripts for their languages came to dwell more and more in an abstract reality. Our thoughts have shifted from residing within a larger living sphere to the limited realms of our minds. We get caught up in thinking, distinct from the embodied experience of the sentient world. This trend has arrived in full force with our current complete dependence on technology, where a person can go for days working, communicating, and being entertained without stepping outside or being in the physical presence of another being. The spaces we inhabit have gone from vast bioregions to invisible cyberspace.

Formalized religion also played a role in our separation from nature. Earth-based cultures typically experience the sacred in the form of spirituality within nature. Trees, mountains, ancestors, rivers, and other entities are imbued with divine wisdom. One does not need to enter a house of worship to experience this, as the sacred is essentially everywhere. While there are certainly spiritual leaders and wisdom holders within earth-based spiritual traditions, everyone has access to firsthand experiences of the divine through their encounters with nature.

In contrast, formal religions are concretized through the written word—in books, through indoctrinated leaders—and take place in houses of worship. The followers of religions experience the sacred secondarily rather than through direct experience. The emphasis here is on controlling religious experience within the confines of powerful religious institutions. These institutions have played roles in subjugating earth-based traditions, often partnering with governments. For example, the witch burnings that took place primarily in Europe, led by the church and governments, resulted in the deaths of hundreds of thousands (up to millions) of pagan peoples (earth-based, small-scale farmers). The bulk of people murdered were women. This process was essentially the internal colonization of Europe, eradicating earth-based Europeans and forcing them to become Christians dependent on the new capitalistic economy. The documentary *The Burning Times* from the Women and Spirituality series is an excellent resource to learn more about this history, as is Silvia Federici's book *Caliban and the Witch: Women, the Body and Primitive Accumulation*.[4]

Another example of religion's role in colonization took place in the Americas, where various European nations, authorized by the church and government, took the lands of First Nations peoples, resulting in collective genocide of

First Nations peoples and often their forced acculturation into Christianity and capitalistic economic life.

Our separation from nature had vast consequences for not only our physical reality but also our psychological, emotional, and spiritual realities. No longer feeling at home within nature, we have been positioned by our new worldview to feel more powerful than nature *and* to feel insecure and fearful of nature. Once again, this mirrors a narcissistic reality where the narcissist sees their self as more special than others, yet also feels insecure. Humans were elevated as the crowning accomplishment of evolution—the masters of the universe, the top of the food chain—yet simultaneously embarked on an oppositional relationship with nature, seeing the natural world as something to be conquered, dissected, destroyed, reconfigured, and exploited. We were no longer family members with the natural world.

## DAMAGED TRUST: REVISITED

Metaphors within various cultures and philosophies teach that Earth is our mother. Often the masculine archetype is held within the sky above and the feminine within Earth. I assume most everyone is familiar with the term *Mother Earth*. Here, the planet—far from being a giant inert rock floating in space—is viewed as an alive presence who loves, nurtures, and protects all the beings living within her. This view was rediscovered within systems science through the work of James Lovelock and Lynn Margulis, who in the late 1960s coined the term *Gaia theory* to express a view of Earth as an alive, intact living system. Many contemporary environmental philosophies have extended this idea, understanding

Gaia (the name taken from Greek mythology) as an earth goddess, our Mother Earth.[5]

The metaphor of Earth as mother is a strong one that translates easily across languages and cultures. While many of the things we associate with mothers may feel stereotypic, most of us can relate to these traits. Each one of us was literally carried in the womb of our mother, dependent on her body for sustenance and care. Her body was our first experience of life, our first ecosystem. Mothers are often characterized as loving and nurturing, holding our well-being and emotions. The archetype of Mother Earth is no different. We are born into this world and live out our lives within the womb of Earth. Everything we need is found within her—water, shelter, food, warmth, the air we breathe, our human companions. Everything arises from Earth.

Yet the way we have chosen to treat Mother Earth does not honor this relationship. Our separation from nature enacts a break with our true mother, Mother Earth, attempting to replace her with the science, rational thought, and materialism we take to be our new caregivers. Since we have moved away from our earth-based traditions, we have embarked on hundreds of years of mistreating our only home. It is not only that we have shifted away from viewing the planet and the beings of nature as sacred and as family members, but we have also been destroying our collective home. As we transitioned away from cultures whose impact on Earth was minimal and in which most of the resources used were replenished, we moved from living in harmony with the planet to a situation where each year we take more and more finite resources. We are in the midst of a mass extinction, with species of plants and animals becoming endangered; tragically, many having gone extinct already. The waters are polluted, from the tiny pieces of plastics pervading the oceans to the toxic chemicals found in rivers, lakes, watersheds, and even our drinking water. The air we breathe is filled with the noxious by-products of fossil fuels, chemicals, massive wildfires, and radioactive waste from nuclear contamination. And human-caused climate change has raised the overall temperature of our planet to unsustainably high levels. Most of us would never treat our human mothers in this manner. In general, we are taught to love and respect our mothers, and they hold very special places in our hearts. But we have lost the understanding that Earth is our mother and instead see the planet as a place to meet our needs, something disposable and inconsequential.

Within the last chapter, we looked at object relations theory and how the attention we receive from our primary caregivers shapes our development. We went over the two troubling patterns wherein a child does not receive sufficient attention: attention withdrawn too early, a lack of attention from the primary caregiver; and excessive early demands, being forced to focus on their primary caregiver's needs rather than their own. Both situations result in the child having damaged trust in people, the world, and themselves. They develop a false self that overaccommodates external expectations.

Many ecopsychologists take our relationship with Earth as a mirror for our levels of psychological and emotional development. The environmental psychologists Deborah Du Nann Winter and Susan M. Koger, whose work was mentioned in chapter 2, connect this relationship to Mother Earth directly with object relations theory.[6] Being cut off from our relationship with Earth, as we often are in our current society, runs parallel to the pattern of attention withdrawn too early. Most children do not have a sufficient relationship with nature. Young children typically spend very little time outside in wild places, which is quite damaging. The author Richard Louv came up with the term *nature-deficit disorder* to describe this phenomenon.[7] He documented how children who do not spend sufficient time in nature commonly develop behavioral problems. Once again, damaged trust is a major result of this pattern.

And this pattern is not confined to our time as children. As noted above, the shift from hunter-gatherer to farming societies initiated major changes in our cultures and our sense of belonging to nature. Over the last several centuries, this shift has gone dramatically further, with a huge proportion of people now living a technology-based existence with very little time spent outside. I often get annoyed at my smartphone when it sends me statistics on how much screen time I spent during the week compared to the week before. I wish instead it would track how much time I spent in nature, as that seems more pertinent.

What about applying the second pattern—excessive needs demands—to the metaphor of Earth as mother? Since our society has severed our healthy relationship with nature, it seems counterintuitive to blame Earth for placing excessive demands on us. Yet climate change and our growing ecological crisis do place excessive demands on us, especially children. Young children who experience floods, wildfires, toxic drinking water, and polluted air often manifest poor health and trauma, and even come to fear nature. As children grow older and learn about the ecological crisis, they can experience additional trauma, pain, sadness, anger, and even apathy. Earth and her systems are suffering, and this suffering is passed on to and includes us.

I also see another way that this second pattern, excessive needs demands, holds in the context of our relationship to nature. In our current society we have essentially removed the role of Earth as mother. We are silencing Earth as a sacred entity and moving into a worldview that no longer experiences Earth as an alive being but rather as a resource for our use. While our familial connection to Earth is always there and can be healed, at present we are not attending to this relationship, and most folks are unaware of the need for it. Not only have we discarded Mother Earth as our primary caregiver but we have replaced her. Instead of having allegiance to Earth, centering our worldview around our home, we have substituted a globalized corporate paradigm that is centered around materialism, hyperindividualism, and, of course, narcissism. In stark contrast to a nurturing Mother Earth, we have been subsumed by a demanding corporate "parent."

As we have seen, the fourth assumption of ecopsychology is that the sickness of humans is embedded in the culture of Western civilization or any culture that is living under corporate globalization. Earlier in this chapter we looked at some of the phenomena that occurred as parts of humanity shifted from our hunter-gatherer traditions to Western civilization. While there are exceptions to the spread of this model, including many Indigenous cultures and trends in many Asian cultures, in general the Western paradigm has spread across the globe through colonization and more recently through corporate globalization.

If you are unfamiliar with the term *corporate globalization*, do not be surprised. It is not something that is often said on radio or television, and certainly not in our day-to-day conversations with friends, family members, and coworkers. Yet corporate globalization is the water we swim in these days—it is always surrounding us. It is exhibited in the nonstop advertisements we receive in our emails, on our smartphones, and via our web searches. It is the slew of never-ending products we buy. It is the control of the economy—our jobs, bank accounts, and ability or inability to purchase vehicles and homes. It has seeped into our political systems and election processes. It is a reality that constantly surrounds us.

Corporate globalization has its lineage in the Western tradition of continual economic expansion. We can trace it to the practices of colonization through which European countries spread across the globe looking for resources, including land and unpaid human labor (enslavement). This marked a surge of power for the nation-state. Previously, power was held in small communities, and our commerce and relationships mostly took place at very small, local levels. As nations consolidated and expanded their power, the economy slowly shifted to a national level and more recently to a global level. Communities no longer met their needs for goods and services locally, living directly off the land through their direct skills. People began to work for others—a larger farmer, a factory, an institution. Today most people work for some institution, and their skills do not directly produce things such as food, clothing, and shelter but rather money to buy these things.

When people are forced from living off the land into a materialistic system, they become both laborers and consumers—and both roles benefit corporations. We have been thrown into a system that we are dependent upon and have little control over. It is an abusive system that has moved us from a mutually reciprocal relationship with nature, including our fellow humans, to one of damaged trust wherein exploitation abounds and we are cut off from our most healthy selves.

✿ ✿ ✿

In witnessing the separation our civilizations have made from Mother Earth, it is important to identify what a healthy relationship with nature might look like. For that I draw once again on the work of Chellis Glendinning, specifically her concept of the "primal matrix." This concept weaves together three qualities that make up the whole of our original state of being that is aligned with nature.[8] The first quality is *"a sense of belonging and security in the world, trust, faith."* So many people do not feel at ease with themselves and certainly do not feel at home within the human and natural world. Glendinning's first quality points to a sense of being at home in our psyches, bodies, communities, and within nature. I relate the second quality—*"a sense of personal integrity, centeredness, capability of I"*—to having a unique purpose in life. Most folks within our culture are raised to "be successful," with a heavy emphasis on material success. A child is encouraged to study hard and engage in curricular activities that translate into getting into a good college so they can obtain a good job. Less consideration seems to be paid to what the child is meant to do—their calling, their gifts—as is emphasized in other cultures and wisdom traditions. These gifts do not necessarily coincide with a high-paying career.

The final quality of the primal matrix is *"the capacity to draw vision and meaning from nonordinary states of consciousness."* Nonordinary states of consciousness or awareness are essentially the experiences that make us say "Wow!" They certainly dip into spiritual experiences, yet they can be relatively simple occurrences: the beauty of seeing the sunrise or catching the full moon; the loveliness one feels when drinking the perfect cup of tea; the contagious laughter shared with a dear friend; the unexpected crossing of paths with a wild animal; the trance that takes you over when you are creating something; the beauty that is often found in the midst of grief. Nonordinary states of awareness are infinite, our birthrights, and generally free of financial cost. Yet the messaging we receive in our society is that the good stuff in life must be bought. The more expensive the better, and we must work hard and compete with others to obtain these things.

In past human societies, Earth was our primary caregiver and the central focus of our existence, and we wove our stories around this relationship to our shared mother. But now we have moved to a new paradigm centered around materialism. We constantly receive messaging that what's important in life is a high status in comparison to others—our wealth, our looks, our jobs, our relationships, our specialness—and that we hold our own in this highly competitive environment. Neither the human community nor the larger Earth community is the important entity—that designation is reserved for the individual.

This worldview is highly profitable for corporations. The

more we care about things tied to consumerism, the more profit corporations receive. When we become self-centered on our false needs, we stop paying attention to the greater needs of the whole. In their groundbreaking essay "The All-Consuming Self" that links consumerism and narcissism, Mary E. Gomes and Allen D. Kanner position the excessive consumerism of people within the United States as an addiction meant to satisfy our false selves.[9] Historically and still today, the advertising industry actually pulls from psychological research to learn many of its tricks. By keeping people feeling deeply insecure about their worth, corporations are able to prey upon these insecurities, and the result is that we constantly purchase goods to try to feel better about ourselves. Face creams, clothing, exercise equipment, new cars, houses, vacations, self-help books, dating apps, you name it—we have become a society that is constantly purchasing things to make us feel worthy. We have become a culture of consumers addicted to our self-images.

In chapter 2 I introduced the concept of the false self in relation to narcissism. A child who experienced one or both of the troubling patterns by their primary caregiver ends up developing a false self—an identity oriented toward meeting the expectations of others rather than understanding their truest wants and needs. This results in adults who are always focused on what others think or see and therefore shift their identities to not only meet but surpass those of the status quo. Living within a society that focuses on materialism, one develops their identity on what materialistic societies desire—expensive things and costly experiences. A narcissist develops this false self and creates an illusionary world where they mirror these externally desirable traits. Within ecopsychology, the false self extends to become an identity that separates ourselves from nature. We take our cues from the civilized world and forget that we are beings meant to live in harmony with Earth, as part of the natural world rather than an exploiter of her.

Our initial separation from earth-based traditions has progressed to our current disconnection under the paradigm of corporate globalization. Most people have either forgotten or never learned our deep intrinsic connections to Earth because we've been taught at a young age to idealize materialism, individualism, competition, and specialness. The deepest needs of our truest selves are not attended to within this paradigm, and we instead continually reach outward for attention. Our focus on these shallow, unnatural traits is turning us into a culture of narcissists.

## ECOLOGICAL NARCISSISM

Having largely disconnected from Earth as our collective primary caregiver and the origin of our ancestral worldviews, we have replaced her with a new parent—the materialistic, competitive, self-centered paradigm of corporate globalization. In the last section we looked at how this dynamic plays out with regard to damaged trust—perhaps the key element in the formation of narcissism. Within this section we will revisit some of the other main traits and patterns of individual narcissism, applying these lenses to our growing collective narcissism to see how they are affecting our relationship with ourselves, one another, and Earth. The destructiveness of our current worldview and practices is severely damaging across these dimensions. By acknowledging and investigating how this plays out in our reality, we can begin to change and heal—a topic addressed further in upcoming chapters.

In chapter 2 we were introduced to the idea of arrested development, where the narcissist who did not accrue a strong sense of self fails to mature and remains psychologically and emotionally stunted at the childhood or, at most, teenage levels of development. Ecopsychology holds the view that our entire culture is in arrested development; the lack of healthy bonding with nature combined with the messaging of consumer culture that most of us received in our early years has left us damaged. Another term for arrested development, although outdated in its language, is *ontogenetic crippling*.[10] Ontogeny refers to the natural development of an organism, and ontogenetic crippling is the stunting of normal development. Both arrested development and ontogenetic crippling directly describe the lack of maturity that results in our perceived separation from the rest of the living world. Although we reach adulthood, at base we remain insecure and act in ways that are overly juvenile, manipulative, and selfish.

In cautioning my students about trusting ideals, individuals, and institutions, I often tell them that there is a difference between an elder and someone who is simply older. In our current culture, we have so many adults who are not necessarily mature or wise. Our focus on getting impressive titles, expensive goods—the "good life"—causes us to concentrate on our own pseudo-needs rather than what is best for the collective whole. In this context, people often view others as means to an end. We are surrounded by leaders (politicians, businesspeople, clergy, educators, gurus) who are predominantly focused on themselves and are unwilling to sacrifice their self-interests for those of the collective whole. The news is constantly breaking stories about shady business deals, corrupt politicians, abusive leaders; we learn more and more that we cannot trust the establishment and, in fact, most people. Most of us have not successfully gone through the rites of passage needed for healthy development. (The depth psychologist Bill Plotkin has some wonderful work in this area that I have listed in our reference section.) What results is that instead of seeing that we are immature and doing the work needed to reach maturity, many of us create a comfortable reality that caters to our needs and subscribes to the overarching culture. The easiest path to happiness seems to be to go with the flow and abide by the norms of the rest of society. Those of us who are fortunate enough to have resources (food, clothing, a home, family, friends, etc.) can swathe ourselves with things and experiences that we believe bring us joy. With abundant consumer choices, we can handpick the objects and events that most closely surround us—our material comforts, where we live, our friends, our media choices—to reflect the identities we wish to have. We can exist in bubbles of ourselves.

Yet even with all the freedom and independence we believe we possess, we cannot eliminate suffering, and our individual and collective pain continues to grow. People living under corporate globalization experience high levels of stress and anxiety. We work long hours to obtain financial rewards, yet many of us are not reaping the benefits of affluence and instead long for more money, we hold uncomfortable amounts of debt, and we are tied to jobs that we do not necessarily enjoy. There is a

prevalence of addictions—to technology (smartphones, appli-
ances, television, video games, etc.), alcohol, drugs, codependent relationships, and, of course, consumerism. Our society
has a host of psychological disorders, including high rates of
depression. Those who live in poverty or with health issues;
veterans of war; those who experience racism, homophobia,
ableism, and other forms of othering; the abused; and the
homeless endure excess suffering. Deep down, many of us
experience existential suffering—the feeling that things are
not as they should be, that we are missing something. We feel
lonely and disconnected to what truly matters. And then there
is the suffering we cause to the planet.

Our society is so obsessed with fulfilling our individual
wants and needs, few of us are truly concerned with the ecological crisis we have created. While on the surface most of us
are aware of climate change and our negative impact on the
planet, we are not radically changing our lifestyles to address
this. Our culture of materialism produced by corporatism is
so strong and oh so comfortable for most of us. Our collective
wounding resulting from experiencing ourselves as separate
and superior to nature, coupled with our adoption of a materialistic, competitive, selfish worldview, is turning us into
a culture of narcissists—which means, in part, a culture of
people whose maturation process has prematurely stopped.

❦ ❦ ❦

In chapter 2, we covered the traits of people with extreme narcissism or NPD: a grandiose sense of self, arrogance, very low
empathy for others, shamelessness, hypersensitivity to critique (fragile ego), and an overall constant need to feel more

special than others. Let us review these one last time—this time in the context of our ecological crisis.

As I've noted several times thus far, the cultural pattern of narcissism, though formed as part of a Western materialistic worldview, now includes many corporatized societies across the globe. For our purposes here, however, we will focus on US society, which seems to embody this pattern most strongly. In this section I will use the abbreviation *US* and the word *American* interchangeably, though I acknowledge that the use of *Americans* to refer to people within the US is problematic since the Americas include North, South, and Central America. The uncritical use of *Americans* to mark the peoples of the United States itself exemplifies a kind of narcissism. I also want to be clear that while I levy many critiques at the US, this is my country of birth, my family has been here for hundreds of years, and despite its many shortcomings, I care deeply about this place and feel we hold so much potential for healing and change. With that said, the US is consistently ranked as having one of the highest ecological footprints in the world. We are well known for our extreme levels of consumerism and waste, and, in general, our country has not been at the forefront of shifting to a more environmentally focused economy or an ecocentric (Earth-centered) mindset.

Most of us are aware that the lands claimed by the US are the original homelands of hundreds of Indigenous tribes (Native Americans/First Nations peoples). When European colonizers and settlers came to this land, they exploited in mass the Indigenous peoples and the land. The colonizers, sanctioned by church and state, viewed these lands as unclaimed. In this they were guided by the principle of terra nullius, which designated the land as free and open for the taking. At the core of this principle was the belief that if people did not extract profit from working the land, they could not claim ownership of it. This Eurocentric and church-dominating land ethic facilitated the divestment of Native Americans of their homelands through genocidal practices and through forcing them onto reservations and coercing them into an acculturated lifestyle.[11] The story that we often tell about America gravely overlooks this reality. Instead, it focuses on a grandiose mythology wherein America's forefathers were brilliant heroes who led a nation of immigrants to these lands and by their sheer strength and ingenuity created a place where anyone could pull themselves up by their bootstraps and become successful. This nationalistic, grandiose sense of self views Americans as the strongest people in the world and as deserving of the affluence we have reaped.

This grandiosity comes conjoined with deep arrogance and entitlement. Manifest destiny—the belief that we were destined to take over all the lands from coast to coast—is a core principle of our story. It is a story of conquest, where it is our right to colonize all the resources of nature for our selfish purposes. We have exploited this land, turning it from wild and abundant forests to agricultural land and then highways, strip malls, endless suburbia, and toxic waste sites. We now have a host of ecological and social issues because of our mistreatment of nature, including humans, yet we are still living under an overall myth that we are the greatest society on Earth. While the US is desirable to so many people around the world because it is seen as a land of opportunity and freedom, we are also seen as extremely arrogant and entitled with the way we treat other nations, our precious resources, and the value of life in general. Our entitlement is exhibited most clearly in our habits of consumption. We fill our homes with so many things that we even have a burgeoning consulting industry on how to reduce the amount of stuff we own. Having things is at the heart of our culture, and we are obsessed with resources—from comforts within our households to the precious resources of Earth. We think little about the waste we expel and the damage we do.

The low level of empathy we exhibit toward the planet directly correlates to our disconnection from Earth. With our silencing of nature, we no longer choose to pay attention to how other species and places are functioning. We are so used to our lifestyles that we often do not question how our habits affect the planet. Yet when this is brought to our attention by the news, ecological disasters, and youth, we often shut down our emotions because we have little bandwidth to face this reality. I cherish the work of the Buddhist philosopher, writer, and activist Joanna Macy. In *Coming Back to Life: Practices to Reconnect Our Lives, Our World*, Macy and her coauthor Molly Young Brown introduce an incredibly helpful list of why we do not look at the ecological crisis.[12] Some of the reasons, as I summarized in a journal article, include "not wanting to experience despair, guilt, and the gloomy reality of the crisis; not wanting to seem anti-American, causing others distress, and seeming irrational, emotional, and weak; or simply associating these feelings with personal problems rather than the state of the world."[13] The feelings that undoubtedly surface when we take the time and energy to recognize what we are collectively doing to the planet are extremely intense. It is not surprising that we repress them, especially since we have already created a fragile reality where we are the central character.

Yet as Macy and Brown also point out, the consequences of ignoring our feelings are great. These feelings are always there below the surface and can result in people having unexplained outbursts of seemingly unrelated emotions, pointing fingers at others rather than taking responsibility for our behaviors, not participating in the political process, refusing to look at the news and other sources of information, decreasing our ability to think and act, and experiencing "burnout" and "powerlessness."[14] The cost of not feeling our emotions toward what is happening to Earth (including ourselves) is high and greatly increases our individual and collective suffering. Within ecopsychology, this pattern is often referred to as *psychic numbing*: the reality of the world seems too heavy, so the individual chooses to remain in illusionary comfort. When we are disconnected from our own emotions, we are also disconnected from our ability to attend to the emotions of other beings. As a numbed-out society, wrapped up in our addictions and trauma, we feel little connection to Earth.

The trait of shamelessness, where one is self-righteous and puts others down to elevate their status, is exhibited in the fixedness our society holds in believing we are superior to other cultures and nature. The process of colonization—moving us from our original earth-based traditions to our current Western globalized framework—has created in us a superiority complex. Earth-based cultures are viewed as primitive—having few luxuries, living in the past, being dirty, holding superstitious beliefs. Within the consumerist mindset, we value simple things as less worthy and cheap as compared to high-dollar items. Why would one choose to live off the land when you can live in a luxury home and dine at fancy restaurants? In other cases, we romanticize earth-based cultures and appropriate them for our uses—in effect, we treat them as commodities through taking their traditional medical plants, ceremonies, and other customs for our benefit. Yet shamelessness masks a deep sense of insecurity, and here the insecurity runs through our lineage, dating back to the time when our own earth-based traditions were eradicated and we were forced into a colonized worldview. To enter this new paradigm, we had to forsake our original sacred connections to Earth.

Lastly, our current societal story, like the personal story of an individual narcissist, is very fragile. It needs to be constantly fueled with a tale of specialness—that we are great, better than others, that we are living the dream. Each moment is filled with stuff—things to do, self-referential thoughts, judgment, criticism, endless purchases, nonstop messaging via our technology. In the moments when we do stop, we often feel an emptiness that we cannot bear, so we resume the continual illusion that we are fulfilled. Our narcissism takes full form in our inability to authentically relate to the larger world, for in doing so our reality might crumble.

## WHITENESS AND COLLECTIVE NARCISSISM

*"Mirror, mirror on the wall, who's the fairest of them all?"*

You are probably familiar with the question above from the beloved fairy tale *Snow White*. The speaker is the evil queen, who is a fabulous archetype of a malignant narcissist. This fairy tale is a classic example of the worldview we are passing on to our youth. Ironically, although the queen comes to a bad end, the moral of the story does not debunk the myth that being fair is a superior state.

I would be remiss, in this book, if I did not bring in the connection between narcissism in our culture and whiteness. One of the key takeaways from the last section is that to enter our Western, materialistic, colonized worldview, our ancestors had to forsake their earth-based traditions. This great loss lies at the heart of our current ecological crisis and growing narcissism. Through the lens of Western materialistic culture, our society views earth-based traditions as primitive and archaic. Our society views people of color similarly, with "the fairer the better" being the norm.

While "American" culture is regarded as a creative and somewhat experimental melting pot held together by principles of freedom, to enter the American dream requires one's acculturation to a homogenizing norm. Giving up one's ethnic traditions and views and entering a culture of materialism are a pattern within US history. When Europeans colonized Turtle Island (the lands we now call the United States), the First Nations peoples of this land were faced with battles, wars, germs, and massacres. As unbelievable as it may sound, the government actually debated whether to kill tribal populations or to acculturate them. While both occurred, acculturation was eventually adopted as a goal, to be effected in part through the establishment of reservations throughout the country along with the horrible and traumatic practice of mandatory boarding schools. Essentially, boarding schools ripped Native American children away from their families, forcing them to go to school away from home; banned their languages, ceremonies, way of dress, and overall culture; and replaced their ways with the traditions of white Europeans. Children were physically and sexually abused, and some went missing or died. Generations of Native Americans were affected, and of course, these cultural and physical assaults profoundly limited their ability to pass on their traditions.

A similar story occurred for the African American descendants of enslavement. Literally stolen from their native lands, these Indigenous peoples were forced into slavery for generations. They were redistributed in a manner that kept them separate from other tribal members, thus unable to use their native languages while they were forcibly turned into unpaid, abused labor for white Europeans. When emancipation finally came, black folks were marginally accepted into low status and forced to acculturate into whiteness.

Although the histories of violent coercion of Native Americans and African Americans are particularly appalling, it is important to know that even Europeans and other people we now consider white were forced to acculturate into whiteness. In fact, whiteness was created to form a superficial solidarity between owning-class whites and the working class and indentured servants descended from Europe. This was done to break any genuine solidarity between poor and working-class Europeans, free and enslaved Africans, and Native Americans. This dynamic is still being played out today.

In a well-known ecopsychology interview, the author, social justice activist, and urban planner Carl C. Anthony breaks down the problematic connection made between purity and whiteness.[15] The Anglo-Saxon archetype has been heralded in the US as the top of the food chain and the model of who we should mirror. It is a sterilized identity that is unemotional, Christian, hierarchical, competitive, and overly focused on cleanliness and purity. This is projected onto the human relationship with the rest of nature, where nature is seen as impure, dirty, meddling, mysterious, and less than. People of color are more closely associated with nature, which positions them as less than. At the core of this is the disassociation people descended from Europe had to make to become white and fit into a colonized identity.

While white people toward the top of the food chain reap material benefits from acquiescing to and participating in the colonial process, gaining profit from the exploitation of both people and nature, people of color and white people toward the bottom do not. The field of environmental justice identifies that people of color, Indigenous people, the poor and working class, women, and children are disproportionately affected by the ecological crisis. These identities bear the brunt of environmental degradation as it falls on humans, though, of course, Earth's systems and nonhuman species receive the greatest damage of all. Various factors are involved here. The communities in which these folks live and the jobs they hold are major factors. Many folks within these groupings work jobs with more environmental risks, such as exposure to toxins in factories, farms, shops, and other industries. Similarly, the places in which these folks live—closer to polluting industries, highways, and other hazards—tend to hold greater environmental risks. They commonly also have fewer resources within their communities because the resources are based on the taxable income of residents, disproportionately affecting poorer communities. For example, where one community may have abundant clean water, another may have outdated pipes that poison the people.

When we relate whiteness to narcissism, it is not meant to correlate all white people as being narcissists but to highlight the system of whiteness wherein becoming and identifying as white parallels our collective narcissism. Here is a little anecdote that may help with this. When I was in middle school, I remember sitting at the dinner table with my parents and my brother and listening to my dad speak. While telling a story about his life and career, he used the phrase "when I became white." He quickly corrected himself, but I remember feeling a little perplexed and have held on to this memory for a long time. While my dad is quite proud to be African American, what he was trying to describe was his acculturation into a successful career and lifestyle—that which is associated with whiteness. While many identify the term *white supremacy* with the most brutal forms of racial violence—it is a system that lays the ground for whiteness within the United States—more broadly it is a form of privilege that functions on the institutional level such that those that fit into the archetype of whiteness typically receive the most benefits.

Whiteness fuels a sense of entitlement mirroring that of narcissism. On this topic, I appreciate the words of the academic Donald E. Collins:

Where American racism and narcissism come together is in the constant urge to maximise advantage over others and satiate the desire for greatness and wealth. This is mixed with a disdain for those who have been deemed lesser and the willful ignorance of the conditions in which they may suffer. In other words, racism and narcissism are two separate yet interdependent constructs.[16]

When we live within a hierarchical society that values whiteness (and straightness) above other identities, those that reap the benefits of whiteness may consciously or unconsciously feel they are better than others. And why wouldn't they? Whiteness tells people with European heritage that they have achieved more, they have higher status, they are uniquely special, and all of this is well deserved. Yet none of this is true. Whiteness is illusory—it is a world that was created to promote a system of hierarchy where some are at the top and others are at the bottom. People of color, Indigenous peoples, and the poor and working class are toward the bottom.

It is important to note that while whiteness and narcissism are related, narcissism is by no means restricted to white people, and in some cases, narcissism exhibits at higher rates in people of color in the US. One example of this is data that shows people of color are getting plastic surgery at higher percentages than whites.[17] The link here is the connection between narcissism, economic class, and the pressure to acculturate. Consumerism continually bombards us with the need for higher status. These messages hit harder on someone who has less, as they see they are lacking according to the accepted standard. Living in a society that devalues one's identity based on skin color, coupled with a devaluing of one's identity based on class, can create a very fragile ego that seeks special attention. For many folks, the key to transcend this devaluation appears to be joining into the culture of whiteness.

The terms *white privilege* and *white fragility* are becoming more widespread. Both convey the problematic nature of being white in a country that is based on systems of oppression, where white people are on top. White fragility is the phenomenon where white people are so insulated from seeing the underlying systems of white supremacy surrounding them that any information or experience that brings this to awareness causes them stress.[18] It is another form of privilege and denial, and it closely resembles narcissism. When you live in a society where you are constantly told by the overarching culture that you are superior based on your skin color, and the societal systems reinforce and encourage this view, you may consciously or unconsciously come to believe it. White fragility is synonymous with entitlement and arrogance, and its name indicates fragility. This sense of fragility experienced by white people in regard to racism runs parallel to the narcissist's fragile ego and hypersensitivity to critique.

Unfortunately, research also indicates that a narcissistic white person is more likely to be racist.[19] A narcissist has created a false identity where their values are right, causing the values of others to be wrong. This sparks a very fixed worldview that can lead to "racism, sexism, nationalism, and classism."[20] There is also a deep fear within white America that the systems of privilege they are accustomed to are currently being dismantled by the Left, people of color, and environmentalists. The medical expert and psychiatrist Tom Singer has introduced the term *extinction anxiety* to refer to the fear white people have over losing their current status.[21]

The Jungian analyst Nancy Furlotti underscores that a person with a fixed, white-black perspective is unable to hold empathy for peoples that are not within their own worldview, since empathy resides in between the different perspectives.[22] The ego fragility of the narcissist who is embedded in a fixed view may appear as rageful outbursts against those they perceive as different and threatening.

❧ ❧ ❧

Our growing culture of narcissism is occurring, in large part, due to the heavy emphasis on consumerism sparked by our desires for greater wealth, specialness, and privilege. US society is based within a capitalistic system that encourages ever-increasing prosperity for the individual and corporation. Our country's history with racism and other forms of oppression is not a secret, and right now these issues are front and center. We have lived a mythological story that coos us into believing that if you work hard, wealth and security are in reach. As more and more folks realize that the "American dream" is no longer obtainable, we question this story more and more. Coupling this with modern racism, many are learning that this country has been based on systems of white privilege where the American dream was structured for those who claimed whiteness, first with being white and upper class, eventually becoming more open to working-class whites (although often not really). Marginalized populations such as people of color—African, Native, Chicana, Latina, and many Asian Americans—have not been included in this dying dream.

When we tie this back to the story of Earth as our mother, we see that silencing peoples of color, Indigenous peoples, poor and working-class whites who were more recently tied to the land further escalates our ecological crisis. These identities are more prone to be keepers of the Earth because their worldviews and well-being are directly tied to the planet. As we continue to minimize and persecute these populations under systems of oppression, our ability to connect with and protect the planet falls.

In the next chapter, we will enter a more experiential level of the false self that has bred our collective narcissism, disconnection from nature, and silencing of our more metaphysical dimensions. This will move us toward many of our causes of suffering from our truest sources and how to face this and reenter these sacred dimensions.

---

## EXERCISE
### EARTH SNOW GLOBE

If you have made it to this point in the chapter, you may be feeling overwhelmed with everything we just unpacked. I know I am. Looking at narcissism, social justice issues, our overarching society, and the ecological crisis is not a light undertaking. I want to thank you for having the courage to unpeel these layers and to stay with this work.

In our previous chapters, I introduced exercises to help support our process. As always, feel free to go back to those and practice them. I was introduced to a practice I found helpful for dealing with the unhealthy feelings I retained from my interaction with a narcissist. The practice is to visualize the narcissist within a snow globe and then shake the globe up, covering them with snow and removing their presence from your world. I offer the following adaptation to shake up the factors that are disconnecting us from our truest worlds.

❦ ❦ ❦

Find yourself a comfortable, quiet space and begin sitting upright. Close your eyes, feel your body settle into your seat, and connect with the ground beneath you. Take a few moments to find your breath, breathing in and out of your nose, letting your inhales start from your belly and rise upward through your torso, heart, shoulders, and crown. Let your exhales descend back down your torso, releasing any thoughts, emotions, and pain you may be feeling.

When you feel somewhat more settled, visualize yourself in a place in nature where you feel safe and that you love. Perhaps this is a spot under a tree in a park or on a beach looking out at the ocean. Do not think too hard about finding the perfect space; just let a place come to you and be there in your mind, heart, and body. Once you are there, imagine you have roots that form at your sit bones and burrow deep into the earth. These roots are incredibly strong and bring you comfort and grounding energy. You feel safe in this space, and these roots support you. The only sounds around you are from nature. There is nothing distracting you.

Now imagine that the space that you are in is encapsulated in a beautiful glass bubble—it is like your own snow globe of earth space. You are in this place in nature that you love and are sitting safely inside. In the distance, you see glimmers of outside factors that flash and disappear. You might see a highway of traffic, a television with the nightly news playing, billboards, a factory with a plume of smoke. Perhaps you see the smoke from wildfire or a flash of melting icebergs. Maybe your images include a protest, a war, sickness, stories from our collective history. Let your mind and heart wander, knowing you are safe inside your Earth globe. Give yourself a few minutes to see what arises and keep breathing deeply.

With the skies outside your Earth globe filled with these flashing images, you suddenly notice that while you are still and connected to Earth through your body and deep roots, the world outside your globe starts to spin. It looks like a dark storm, and the images whirl around outside your globe, becoming blurrier and blurrier. After a minute or two of swirling like a strong windstorm, they disappear.

Allow yourself to sit for a few more minutes (or as long as you like) in this stillness and space of connectedness. Notice how it feels, and keep breathing. When you feel ready, open your eyes slowly and come back to your space. You may want to journal for a few minutes about this experience.

# 4

—

# THE FALSE SELF

At this point in our journey, we have covered a great
deal of ground—building a strong understanding of
narcissism as both a personality disorder and a collective trend affecting our society, as well as seeing how our
collective narcissism is negatively affecting our well-being,
our communities, and the entire planet. Staying with this
material takes a lot of courage and compassion, so I thank
you for showing up in this way. As we have seen, narcissism
works to create a reality that is very closed and focused on
one's individual, limited self-interest—it is a crisis of self-
absorption. The work we are doing here does the opposite; it
expands our awareness so we can see the harm we are doing
collectively. This awareness is a necessary precursor to moving in a healthier direction.

In this chapter, we will shift to a more interior, metaphysical focus, looking at questions of self. After revisiting the false

self, we will explore the movement toward a more authentic self, consider the possibilities of a larger Self, and use the concept of the "daemon" (also referred to as "daimon") to see what barriers stand in the way of our realization. Finding our true selves is an important key in healing the damage we are doing to all beings of Earth.

Throughout this book, we have looked at the problem of the growing narcissism in our society, including the specific traits and patterns of extreme narcissism and narcissistic personality disorder, translating these characteristics to the collective narcissism we are witnessing within corporate globalized societies. A main point is that while individual narcissism is real and problematic, it is our collective narcissism that is doing the greatest damage to ourselves and all living beings. With our work here, we are not attempting to fix individuals who hold clinical diagnoses of NPD; rather, we are addressing our overarching society that is inundated with self-centeredness, resulting in little care for other humans and Earth. We are looking at narcissism as a societal problem that is spurred by the consumerist, capitalistic culture of Western civilization and any culture that has been co-opted by global corporatization. By doing so, we begin to understand that this larger culture is breeding us to be narcissistic because narcissistic populations are profitable, and the result is damage to ourselves and Earth. In becoming aware of the smoke and mirrors, we begin to see what lies behind them. Part of this work involves a further exploration of our problematic ideas and practices of self and restructuring these into healthier ones that participate with, rather than against, the larger living systems of life, the collective whole.

*Who am I? Where do I begin and end? From where does my self arise?* I suspect by your choice to read this book that these are questions you have asked at some point in your life. These are quintessential questions that do not necessarily have fixed, final answers. The questions themselves set the journey.

## THE FALSE SELF REVISITED

Previous sections of this book introduced us to the idea of the false self. While the original notion of a false self came out of the field of pediatric psychoanalysis and focused on child-parent relationships, an ecopsychology perspective allows us to extend the concept to show how we develop in order to fit into Western global corporate culture. Living within a culture that tells us we have more worth if we are wealthy, physically attractive, and generally doing better than others breeds us to be competitive and to constantly acquire things and experiences that we do not necessarily want or need. Essentially we are presented with an archetype of who we should be that is set by a nonsensical standard.

Although the ecopsychology perspective on the false self applies equally to adults, it does not negate the importance of childhood development in this process. Early childhood is an extremely important window in which we can learn to trust ourselves, other people, and nature. Early childhood is when we begin to develop skills and learn what we like and what we are good at, and when we become aware of the beauty, joy, and awe of our momentary experiences with life. With the constant pressure from formidable systems of Western civilization that breed insecurity, mistrust, disconnection, standardization, and constant distraction from our direct experience, many of us either never develop that healthy sense of self in childhood or we grow out of alignment with it as we age. The result is the development of a false self that constantly focuses on the outward needs peddled to the individual by our superficial society.

The narcissistic personality and the false self correlate closely. Though not everyone who exhibits a false self is narcissistic, people who are extremely narcissistic have false selves. As you may recall, the wounding they received in early childhood caused them to create an alternate reality where they are in control and have safe boundaries. Things that are threatening or do not conform to the narcissist's fixed categories of good and right are not allowed to enter their world. When someone or something violates the narcissist's false reality, they are expelled from it by the narcissist. In addition, the narcissist is highly insecure and has little ability to handle critique, which they counterbalance with an overblown sense of self, arrogance, and a constant need to feel special. The narcissist's fragility results in a false self—a fictitious reality where they are the center of everything. The narcissist often has no to low awareness of their dynamic and sees others, rather than themselves, as being problematic.

Similar to the narcissist, many of us living within a capitalistic Western corporate society that keeps us hyperfocused on image, competition, and consumption feel comfortable prioritizing our desire for wealth and other forms of status above others. We have collectively become comfortable with the thought that we are the center of the universe, that our needs and stories are more important than anything else. Even those of us who do not subscribe to the idea that we are of paramount importance often accept the materialistic reality, this false reality, as normal, and we arrange our lifestyles and values to accommodate this. In looking at how the false self damages Earth, we see that individuals who are constantly trying to meet their needs through forms of consumption, accumulation, and individual pursuit engage in activities that produce high levels of waste and little concern for the welfare of other beings. The false self is detrimental to the individuals who hold one for these are defined by a deep sense of emptiness and a longing for something that eludes them.

At the heart of a false self is a deep sense of loneliness and despair. It is a feeling of lack wherein even the acquirement of things, experiences, and people does not fulfill us. There is a sense—sometimes conscious, but more often unconscious—that something is missing. One comparison to this state is what happens when a person has plenty to eat yet the food they are consuming is not nutritious. One can eat and eat and feel full in a physical sense but there is no sense of satisfaction from the body being nourished. Moreover, this way of eating results in poor health, a pathway to a slow death, often without even knowing it. Many of us do not have the context of what we are doing to ourselves because so much of the larger story tells us that the more we consume what we desire, the better off we will be.

To dispel this myth requires waking up to something deeper and truer that arises within our most authentic selves as well as in the larger world. A primary route to this awakening is through connecting with nature, including the human community. This waking up is much of the focus of ecopsychology, and more and more people are turning in this direction.

In "The All-Consuming Self," Mary E. Gomes and Allen D. Kanner offer a three-step process for working with a narcissistic personality that applies to the greater societal narcissism we are witnessing.[1] The first step is to help the individual see that they are living within a false self. There are many forms of doing this. Often exposure to information that documents the pain and suffering we are causing to the planet and to ourselves can kick-start the process of seeing that something is wrong and prompt us to ask bigger questions. This is the stage of waking up to the ecological crisis, seeing that there is a problem, and perhaps starting to understand that our individual views and actions contribute to this problem. While information alone does not necessarily change someone, it can spark deeper questioning. When we look at the statistics documenting the damage and apprehend the underlying suffering that is occurring as a result of our ecological and human crises, our thoughts and emotions are triggered and most likely we experience pain for the world and for ourselves. We begin to see that we are living under a false reality that is causing harm, and we may become distraught, angry, depressed, apathetic, or even despondent.

The second step addresses the difficult emotions that surface as a result of waking up to the ecological crisis and allowing our false self to be identified and start to dissipate. The work of Joanna Macy as well as many ecopsychologists addresses this emotional and psychological pain. At the crux of their approaches is actually feeling the pain, being with it rather than trying to deny it. When we can stay with the pain, with support from others (including the more-than-human natural world), we eventually hit rock bottom and become empowered to make substantial changes in our views and actions that align more with the health of all beings. The final step is all about this—finding what our deeper values, desires, and skills truly are and how to apply these to a healthier life path. As radical environmental writer Derrick Jensen writes, "By confronting the problem as courageously as we can and at the same time presenting alternatives, our barriers to clarity, including our false hopes, may crumble to reveal previously unseen possibilities."[2]

## THE SELF

Having looked in-depth at the false self, it is time to ask, what is the real self? This is a very abstract, philosophical question, as the self does not exist in a bounded container. The self cannot be pinpointed to our mental activity, our feelings and sensations, or our spirit or soul; yet the self includes all these dimensions and more. The self is also an embodied experience. So much of our identity is created by what we do and feel—the sensations of having a body, the joy and despair of love and life.

So far in this book, I have used the term *ego* in relationship to narcissism—in this context, the ego refers to our construction of our identity. Ego is our expression of self-worth, our self-esteem. Narcissists typically display big, arrogant egos, yet underneath the display their egos are often fragile, reflecting deep-seated insecurity. If you have studied psychology, particularly Freudian psychology, you probably have a more particular definition of ego, where the ego is the rational component of the personality. This ego executes limits on the personality so it can function.

Now I would like to add a new context for the term *ego*. Within Buddhism, the ego or illusory sense of self is often seen as the root of all suffering, as it continually causes us to become attached to our identities and experiences. From a Buddhist standpoint, ego is problematic because it constructs a dualistic view in which abstract thinking, the physical body, and emotions are taken to be *me*, while outward things are *not me*. We claim ownership of our identity, creating a boundary that shuts out larger experiences, falsely thinking we are separate from them. If you recall, ecopsychology has a similar view where our disconnection from nature and orientation to a separate self cause collective suffering. Buddhism and ecopsychology thus hold views of ego or self that derive from a metaphysics quite different from that in mainstream Western thought. These alternative metaphysics look at the nature of the mind as not only the human mind but also a larger mind or consciousness that connects and even transcends all beings and experiences.

Within an ecopsychological framework, the individual and nature are not separate but expressions of the same phenomenon. Within Buddhism, our individual self and all phenomena, both seen and unseen, are connected. To end one's suffering, one needs to move toward egolessness, or a no-self. We'll now look at two aids for doing this—a teaching from classical Buddhism and a model of the self drawn from transpersonal studies and ecopsychology.

## The Skandhas

At some point in their training, most Buddhist meditation practitioners are exposed to what are called the *skandhas*, or the five aggregates. These concepts can seem fairly elusive, as they help to define questions of what the self is and what the self is not without ever really answering these questions. The purpose of teaching these skandhas is for the meditation practitioner to become less attached to self, to both see and let go of this identity. My experience with contemplating the skandhas is a sense that varying aspects of me that I genuinely know are both real and unreal. It is almost like having the epiphany that every aspect of my body and mind will one day be gone, yet there is some part of what I am experiencing that is everlasting—but it cannot be claimed as me. While I am a long-term meditation practitioner and a certified meditation instructor, I make no claims on enlightenment or even any mastery of these ideas. But I find them extremely important in order to contemplate the self, so let's take a look.

The skandhas are five lenses of experience that are connected and that build upon one another. *Skandhas* is often translated as "aggregates," which can be helpful to envision since aggregates are the various elements that combine to form a whole. The skandhas are the various elements that create the self, yet these elements are often fleeting, as they consistently change. These five skandhas include (1) our physical perceiving forms (eyes, ears, nose, tongue, body, and mind), (2) the sensations experienced by these various forms, (3) the perceptions that are formed between our sensing body and outward phenomena, (4) our construction of thoughts, and (5) the consciousness we create by bringing all these skandhas together. Within the context of an egoic self, the skandhas essentially work to concretize our sensory experiences and perceptions into a fixed reality. But within the concept of a perceptually open and aware self, the skandhas help to transform the illusion of a fixed self and fixed reality. Most of us, instead of taking the time to experience the openness of the moment with our senses, overlay each moment with preconceived notions. This results in a very fixed, egoic sense of self whose quickness to collapse perceptions and experiences into familiar labels reinforces what we believe to be our experiences and identities.

I have an example of this that I often recall to my students. Years ago, I was at a retreat for my doctoral program in California. It was a beautiful day, and my cohort of peers and teachers went on a hike. A dear friend and I ended up walking a bit ahead of the group and, at some point, stopped at a remarkable tree stump. We were both struck by it and stood there staring at its immense circumference and hollowness. As I looked into the tree stump, I could see a pool of deep, dark water reflecting little bits of light, as well as threads of cobwebs strewn across. Suddenly my friend remarked that it was large enough that we could both fit into the tree base and suggested we hide within it and pop out and surprise the group when they caught up to us. I remember looking up at him thinking he was odd and a bit crazy—I did not want to get into a pool of dark, cold water.

And then I looked again, and the tree stump was dry and empty: there was no water. That moment continues to amaze me because I see how I was overlaying a false reality onto my experience. Upon reflection I realized that a previous experience while visiting a forest in Lebanon had primed me to see a water-filled tree stump. I had created a reality based on an outdated experience, thus blocking an authentic encounter with the present. Yet in seeing this, I ended up having an authentic experience of the present.

Although my experience with the tree stump is in one sense quite simple and ordinary, it remains shocking to me as an example of our ability to create a false reality and believe it so strongly. It makes me wonder how often I do this without even knowing. The awareness of our habitual division between our present-moment experiences and the fixed reality we have created is essential to breaking our negative patterns with the skandhas. When we can minimize the duality of experiencing the self as preconceived and instead open our awareness to what actually is without too much meta-narration, our self develops a fluidity. The Buddhist *Heart Sutra* has beautiful and profound ways of deconstructing our attachment to fixed elements of our self, counseling "no eye, no ear, no nose, no tongue, no body, and no mind"—there is nothing we can definitely claim as our self. The irony is that when we let go of this attachment to self, we find a Self that arises and connects with all of life.

### The Ecological Self and Self with a Capital S
Transpersonal studies is an academic field comprising multidisciplinary inquiries that include and extend beyond the person to incorporate broader experiences of life, even metaphysical realms. Within that field, people often speak to the difference between a self with a lowercase *s* and a Self with a capital *S*. The former refers to the small, ego-based self of the individual, while the latter describes a much larger Self that extends to all beings and even all phenomena. The *ecological self*, an identity discussed in ecopsychology and deep ecology,

closely resembles the Self as discussed in transpersonal studies. The ecological self was first identified by the Norwegian philosopher Arne Naess, the founder of deep ecology.[3] The ecophilosopher and activist Joanna Macy has given the phrase a more active feeling by calling it "the greening of the self."[4] Naess would also refer to it as the process of self-realization, as it is a means of maturing from the small ego self to a sense of self that is in relationship with the more-than-human natural world.

The ecological self develops our understanding that we are connected to nature, building our recognition that we feel compassion and even love for nature. While you may not have heard of the ecological self prior to this, you probably can identify your ecological self. It is the experience you have in a place in nature that brings you peace and joy: sitting on a beach looking out at the horizon, walking along a trail while the fall leaves crunch under your feet, seeing the first sprout from your garden, feeling the warmth of a fire on a very cold day, spotting a passing herd of deer, getting soaked in the first summer rainstorm, hearing birdsong—the possibilities are endless. The ecological self broadens our identity to encompass nature; it sparks caring and an understanding that we are in this life together, rather than separate.

The Self with the capital S is quite similar to the ecological self, yet it goes even further. It extends into all aspects of the seen and unseen world, from all beings on Earth, to all places, to our psyches, to our shared psyches, to our dream world—it reaches everywhere. Many people think of this Self as a mystical or spiritual reality, but it can also be approached without those views. It is the ground of all being—a force that connects all life. Though such an all-encompassing force can't be reduced to one field of study, one often finds it in the realms of metaphysics, philosophy, and consciousness studies. The famous early-twentieth-century psychiatrist Carl Jung called the Self the *collective unconscious*, describing a psyche shared by all phenomena. When we recognize this Self, we begin to glimpse our shared life with all beings.

The concept of the Self is much deeper and more complex than I am presenting it here. It is the subject of endless books, wisdom traditions, and practices. The point here is to bring the Self into our exploration of collective narcissism and its remedies. We have seen that most people within our society are in a state of arrested development, meaning they remain stuck at an immature level. A healthy sense of self opens the door for the ego to mature into a social self (a self that takes others' needs and perspectives as valid and important) and perhaps further to the ecological self and ultimately to the bigger Self. We desperately need more of us to engage this process of maturity in order to address our collective suffering and to begin healing.

It is important to note that this bigger Self is extremely threatening to the narcissistic individual, as accessing it requires them to let go of their fixed sense of identity, their ego. Since the narcissistic personality has a fragile ego, they will put considerable energy into maintaining their world and exerting control over it. To access the Self requires letting go of this control and allowing in a greater intelligence. This Self includes our individual wisdom and transcends it, accessing wisdom from countless forms. To access this Self necessitates grace—an openness to something much, much bigger. This does not have to be "God" or some divine being, yet if it is helpful to think of it as this, that is all good. For me, as someone who grew up watching *Star Wars* movies, I sometimes find myself—chucklingly—employing an analogy of this Self, this grace, as "the force." It is essentially the water we swim in, yet so many of us do not see it, acknowledge it, or let it shape our reality. Our Self is a form of help, yet when we block it out, we cause problems for ourselves and for all beings. When we do let in our Self and grow, we gain a wise guardian or guide.

It can be helpful to envision this Self as a body of water that arises and falls like a wave. As the wave rises, it is shaped by various independent elements that join together to form, and then suddenly the wave dissipates. Our Self arises from a collection of what Buddhists often call *dependent co-arisings*, which acknowledges that nothing is separate and distinct and that we are mutually dependent upon all phenomena for both creation and dissolution. The various selves of all phenomena form this greater Self, and this greater Self is both everything and nothing. Like the wave, it rises and falls and rises again. When we begin to apply this metaphor to our smaller selves, we begin to see the futility of our attachments and perhaps start to let go of holding a fixed, constant reality as well as a need to maintain a large sense of ego.

## THE DEMON OF EGOCENTRICITY

Having now looked at a number of negative associations regarding the egoic self, I want to reemphasize the importance of having a healthy sense of self, a healthy ego. In fact, a healthy ego is necessary in maturing toward the larger kinds of self or Self discussed above. In our opening chapter, we took note that everyone has certain levels of narcissism, and this is healthy. The problem of having an unhealthy ego, an extremely narcissistic self, arises when our sense of self is overblown yet fragile. In that state we are overly controlling of our reality, to the extent that we cannot be vulnerable and open to other beings and experiences. We are stuck.

Earlier I noted that in Buddhism, the ego is often seen as the root of all suffering, as it continually causes us to become attached to our identities and experiences. Although our attachments are often painful, they are also comfortable and reliable and so many of us are fearful of remaining in the present moment without them. For those of us with some familiarity with Buddhism or meditation practice, this idea is probably not new. There are so many extraordinary resources for loosening attachments both abstractly and through practice. Like many others, I am smitten with the teachings and presence of Pema Chödrön. Years ago, I was standing in a checkout line at a grocery store where I live in Boulder, Colorado. Checking out with a cashier a couple lines over, I saw a white woman with a shaved head, wearing Buddhist robes. I looked at her closely, not only because she stood out but also because I assumed I would know her through the Naropa University community and the local meditation scene. The woman turned my way, looked at me, nodded her head, and smiled. It was only after this moment that I realized it was none other than Pema Chödrön herself. I always remember that moment, as I felt so honored and acknowledged in my own humanity by someone who did not have to take this time to do so.

Through her lineage teachings, Chödrön often addresses our attachment to ego and our *stuckness*. She has a very concise and illuminating definition of ego as "the experience of never being present."[5] When we drop into the present moment, we are confronted with feeling our feelings, dealing with what is going on for us emotionally and psychologically. We cannot cloak ourselves in stories from our past, fantasies about the future, or the persona we wish to project. It is an unraveling that is very scary to most of us because we feel out of control. Meditation teaches us to work not only with the fears that arise but also with the unexpected beauty of the present moment. Chödrön has rephrased the Buddhist concept of *shenpa*, or "attachment," as "hooked," to express the habitual ways in which we become fixated on our ego identities. Similar to the narcissistic personality, being hooked is to cling closely to our false selves that were constructed to protect ourselves from perceived threats from the larger world. The activity involved in this becomes all consuming, a self-absorption that blocks out the experience of the present, including our deeper selves; the shenpa is the frantic energy behind this, and it causes suffering.

The fundamental, most basic shenpa is to ego itself: attachment to our identity, the image of who we think we are. When we experience our identity as being threatened, our self-absorption gets very strong, and shenpa automatically arises. Then there is the spin-off—such as attachment to our possessions or to our views and opinions. For example, someone criticizes you. They criticize your politics, they criticize your appearance, they criticize your dearest friend. And shenpa is right there.[6]

If you are anything like me, you probably have endless experiences with being hooked. Life seems to constantly give us the opportunity to feel this sense of overblown ego attachment, this fear, this frenetic energy. I find it arises most strongly when I am in conflict with someone and my sense of worldview and identity is challenged. Perhaps I receive critical feedback by an authority in a manner that I feel questions my skills and leadership. Perhaps it arises when a family member or friend fails to provide me with the attention I desire. To be honest, I notice that it arises most strongly when I have a conflict within a romantic relationship that I fear is conditional, not guaranteed to last forever. In these moments I feel a range of emotions—fear, rage, confusion, and sadness—sometimes to the extent that I feel immobilized to act in a wise manner.

According to Chödrön, the antidote to this stuckness is to simply engage in this experience, to stay with the fear and discomfort, to actually feel it without moving to a response or action. By doing so, we reconnect with our primal state, what her teacher (and Naropa's founder) Tibetan Buddhist Chögyam Trungpa Rinpoche referred to as "basic goodness." This concept is elusive to me, as it has many interpretations. Chödrön refines basic goodness to the three qualities of "natural intelligence, natural warmth, and natural openness."[7] From my perspective, these are the qualities that arise when we make contact with our present state with trust, in a manner that involves the Self. We experience a ground of being that extends our sense of wisdom, compassion, and awareness beyond our small sense of ego to one that connects with the greater life force of all beings. Basic goodness also reminds me of the concept of the primal matrix that we looked at in our last chapter. This is our natural state of being that occurs when we connect with the larger natural world. In it we experience trust, belonging, and a unique and skillful sense of self, and we find the extraordinary within the present moment.

Pema Chödrön associates our fear of being with our selves without getting hooked by our story lines with the notion of facing our monsters and demons. For years I have been fascinated by our society's fixation on monsters and demons. So many of our popular books, television shows, and movies feature werewolves, vampires, witches, zombies, aliens, and other monsters that lurk on the edges of society, plotting harm. To rid our world of them, we have superhero archetypes who show up just in the nick of time. These various demons represent a threat to our realities, yet in deeper significance the demons are actual aspects of ourselves that we do not wish to see. In contrast, the superhero seems to represent this powerful character that comes in to save us, allowing us to not have to do any of the work. While the superhero may too represent unseen characteristics within ourselves, such as our sense of specialness and fierce individualism, this figure seems to embody more our desire to let go of agency and responsibility and let someone else take care of things. The demon of egocentricity arises when we become self-obsessed but not self-aware—we become self-absorbed, creating a fictitious reality that always allows us to look good through our own reflections yet without genuine confidence. It is when we become so closed-minded and insular that we cut ourselves off from the larger forces of life, including our Self.

## Daemon

While most of us are familiar with the term *demon* as something bad, relating to the devil or really anything that is both menacing and supernatural, far fewer people are familiar with the term *daemon*. I remember the first time I heard this word, in the movie *The Golden Compass*, which is based on the first book of Philip Pullman's *His Dark Materials* trilogy. In the movie, each human character has an animal, or rather a daemon, who is intrinsically tied to them as a protector and guide. If you watched the *Game of Thrones* series, this is similar to the dire wolf each of the Stark children were connected to. In these stories, the daemon is a deeper aspect of the self that has manifested in an animal protector. As someone who often lives with a wolfish-looking dog, I love this idea—that my animal companion is part of my soul, a protector, guide, and friend.

Yet the origins of a daemon are deeper than fictional stories. Daemons are archetypes that show up in a range of cultural origins that were often lost through the process of colonization. The word *daemon* or *daimon* has roots in Ancient Greek and "originally referred to a person's guiding spirit."[8] The daimon was essentially a part of us that appeared in a form separate from us and was both wise and helpful. The famous psychologist James Hillman viewed the daimon as an entity each human received and that manifested prior to one's birth. He claimed each person was imprinted with a unique calling, a destiny, which we forgot upon birth. However, our daimon, which Hillman referred to as our "soul-companion," remembers this and helps guide us to realize our calling.[9] As earth-based traditions were lost through the process of colonization, the daimon was repackaged as a demon. The idea of a daimon would be a threat to the church and the state, as it represented one's ability to have personal authority separate from them, diminishing their power. This process of replacing a familiar concept within an earth-based tradition with a different association that still has some resemblance is common. For example, most of the celebratory days within pagan Europe were replaced with holidays that had a resemblance, such as the winter solstice with the Christian tradition of Christmas. So many works bring together the figures of angels and demons—the connection between the daimon and demon is similar, with the angel correlating with the daimon. Colonization marred the role of the daimon, taking away personal and spiritual power from the individual.

The colonized daemons, as demons, became menacing, dangerous, and fearful creatures. While only seen in physical form within works of fiction, they were given credence within formal religions in the form of the devil and other malevolent characters. A demon is often projected as a bad entity that can gain control over us, such as possession. Clearly most people want nothing to do with them or any realities that integrate the existence of demons. We are really just touching upon demons in their relation to daimons. Both concepts are much more complex than I am presenting them here, and I do not mean to dismiss the existence of real demons in the world as held by many traditions. For example, both Buddhist and Egyptian traditions hold a host of complex demons. My point in bringing in demons is to illustrate how the daimon, a helpful guiding force for our self and Self, was turned into a demon, often silencing our understanding that we have an ally constantly with us.

If we entertain the possibility that each of us has a daimon, a higher Self, in silencing this Self we lose our connection to both our unique callings and a source of invaluable guidance. Moreover, if this daimon is truly a part of us, we are silencing ourselves—repressing much of our gifts, intuition, and sense of trust in the world. Many believe that it is the repressing of these aspects of ourselves that manifests as our demons. We see these demons in the embodied characters of the seven deadly sins—wrath, greed, sloth, pride, lust, envy, and gluttony. Hillman was quite adamant that even if we silence our daemon, it will not disappear—we will eventually need to reconcile or reckon with it. The reconciliation is paying attention to the unique call of our Self and following this guidance, while the reckoning is the negative personality traits that surface as a result of trying to silence authentic parts of ourselves.

The psychotherapist Ralph Metzner described Buddhist demons as representative of the inner aspects of our selves that "are dominated by feelings of pride, jealousy, and anger."[10] We also see demons within the Buddhist three poisons of greed, hatred, and delusion. I find it interesting that these demon qualities closely resemble those held by extreme narcissists. By adhering to the deadened reality of a colonized world, which excludes the possibilities of a more transpersonal reality, we silence a greater Self and concretize a reality fixed on rationality and individuality. This reality breeds an overreliance on the small ego, keeping us stuck in our false self, a false reality. By silencing and not heeding our daemon, or larger Self, we create problems for our self and the larger world.

I am fascinated by the work of the beloved Buddhist teacher Lama Tsultrim Allione, who has created a process for reconciliation that she calls "feeding your demons" (the title of one of her books).[11] Lama Tsultrim claims, "A demon means anything which hinders liberation."[12] The process she has created stems from the writings of Machig Labdrön, a Buddhist teacher from the eleventh century who was female, which was extremely rare for this time period. Relating to the turning of daimons into demons, Lama Tsultrim views demons as our "inner enemies"—those that work against our authentic selves, creating problems and barriers to our life path. I have had the privilege of getting a small taste of this approach to practice at Tara Mandala, Lama Tsultrim's retreat center in Colorado, but my description will not do this very compelling and powerful work justice. Feeding your demons is the work of turning the demon into an ally for the self—bringing this outer aspect of your Self to once again align with your intentions in a way that the demon becomes a guiding form of support once again. At the heart of this is listening to your demon—attending and responding to your own fears, and most pointedly placating your demon through a metaphoric and literal feeding, a supplication. The final aspect is then letting this all go, to momentarily pause your ego fixations within a meditative state. By our witnessing and nurturing of our demons, they shift back into our powerful allies.

❀ ❀ ❀

I know we have come down a path that may be unexpected—from looking at the narcissistic ego to placating our demons. If reading about demons and daimons makes you uncomfortable, this is normal and perfectly okay. The point is not to scare anyone away but to look deeper at the collective self-centeredness we are witnessing within our narcissistic society and to offer the possibility of shifting away from a false self and toward a Self that is healthy. When we are bound to the constraints of our fixed individualism that we alone have the power to control, we are missing out on gaining help and guidance from larger forms. When we entertain the possibility of a larger Self—intelligent, compassionate, and spacious—that is connected to all of life, we may begin to gain a vision of trust in life and a feeling of belonging and purpose. The world may become less frightening if we realize that there is a ground of being that is supportive and meaningful, and that our lives have a calling.

---

### EXERCISE

## THE RAIN SHOWER

Once again, settle yourself in a comfortable, quiet space, and sit upright. If possible, do this outside in a peaceful place. Close your eyes, feel your body settle into your seat, and connect with the ground beneath you. Take a few moments to find your breath. Breathing in and out of your nose, letting your inhales start from your belly and rise upward through your torso, heart, shoulders, and crown. Let your exhales descend back down your torso, releasing any thoughts, emotions, and pain you may be feeling.

With your eyes still closed, imagine yourself in a beautiful park. It is a warm, sunny day, yet there are very few people around. No one can see you where you are sitting on the grass. You feel at peace, breathing in and out, feeling the warm air around you, hearing the sounds of birds singing, and smelling a freshness that invokes summertime. You have a lingering sense of your various thoughts and identities; they are floating high above you. You don't really remember them, but you know they are there.

Suddenly you smell rain. Next, you hear soft raindrops in the distance, and finally you start to feel very gentle, warm rainfall on your head, arms, and lap. The rain feels really good—you do not mind the wetness; it feels cleansing and comforting. With your eyes still closed, you notice that the lingering thoughts and identities that have been floating high above you are being gently dissolved by the rain. Like a raindrop on a windowpane, each thought and identity gets swollen with water and slowly slides to the ground and is absorbed. Slowly but surely the rainfall dissolves all your thoughts and identities. You feel so free, your body feels so alive, you radiate from the inside out, like a light. And suddenly your body becomes points of light, like a swath of fireflies. Each light also becomes swollen with water and eventually falls to the ground. You dissolve into the earth, feeling the deepest sense of peace you have ever felt.

# 5

—

# TOWARD HEALING SELF
# AND PLANET

*If you want to be important—wonderful. If you want to be recognized—wonderful. If you want to be great—wonderful. But recognize that he who is greatest among you shall be your servant. That's a new definition of greatness. By giving that definition of greatness, it means that everybody can be great, because everybody can serve. . . . You only need a heart full of grace, a soul generated by love.*

**—MARTIN LUTHER KING, "THE DRUM MAJOR INSTINCT"[1]**

*Does the bamboo feel jealous of the oak because it is bigger and its leaves change color in the fall? The very idea of the two trees comparing themselves to each other seems ridiculous, but we humans seem to find this habit very hard to break.*

**—OSHO ZEN TAROT[2]**

Throughout this book, we have looked at the dynamics surrounding the collective narcissism we are currently witnessing and how these dynamics are incredibly damaging to ourselves, our communities, and Earth. While narcissism is often situated as an individual disorder, we have developed a larger perspective that recognizes it as a collective disorder affecting most of us. This disorder is due in part to a lack of healthy relationships within our early childhoods, and it may help us to develop empathy for those with extreme narcissism to understand the likelihood that they suffered neglect or trauma in their pasts. I have argued, however, that narcissism is even more commonly perpetuated by a Western system of corporate globalization that has turned us into overly individualized, insecure consumers.

Everyone loses within this system, even those who seem to be winning. On the individual level, we experience a deep sense of loneliness, separation, and insecurity that extends to our lack of connection to community or a sense of belonging. From the widest lens, our collective narcissism causes us to hyperfocus on our individual interests, to be selfish, forsaking our reciprocal relationship with nature and heightening the devasting impact we are having on our home, Earth. In this final chapter, we will engage a question lovingly phrased by my dearest mentor, Belvie Rooks, and her beloved husband, Dedan Gills: "What does healing look like?"[3]

Healing is a dynamic space—the work of healing requires continual attending to our awareness, our relationships, and our actions. And healing appears in a myriad of forms. It does not look like one thing, and there is no set formula for healing. It is a space that is always accessible, yet one that is never set in stone. With the short attention spans we have cultivated in our consumer society, we often want easy answers—the five-point bullet list or prescription refill that will make all of our problems go away. Yet healing is an active process—it is a constantly changing state that comes about through continual awareness, reflection, and practice.

In this chapter, as we look at healing the damage our collective narcissism is doing at various scales and registers, I offer patterns and qualities that are part of this active process. While these qualities may appear distinct, all of them are connected and inseparable from the healing pathway. Please keep in mind that healing will look differently for each of us, yet attending to these qualities can greatly contribute to both our individual and collective processes of healing. Rather than offer a single exercise at the end of the chapter, as I have done so far, in this chapter you will encounter three exercises interspersed throughout. These are intended to help you begin engaging the work of healing actively as you read. To begin, we will look at an aspect of healing that we have already been doing throughout this book, which is waking up to what's happening and allowing that awareness to affect our views and behaviors.

## THE UNRAVELING

Waking up and acknowledging both our individual and collective entrenchment within a narcissistic worldview are a major step toward healing. As we have seen throughout this book, our larger consumer culture wants us to be self-focused. A self-centered orientation conditions us to continually purchase goods and services that add to the growth of the corporate economy and keeps us within a narrow vision that does not question larger economic, political, and social systems or the ecological health of our planet. To change our limited views, we must disrupt our worldview and admit there is a problem. This process comes in many names and forms. For those of us familiar with recovery terminology, it is the process of "hitting rock bottom"—due to our various addictions, we recognize that life as we are currently living is unbearable and not working. It is a process of admitting this and turning the problem over to a larger system that we are not in control of but that invites us to participate within it. It is about being able to see our problems, feel the discordant thoughts and emotions we experience, and seek help. Often it is surrendering to the sense of powerlessness we might feel, which entails stopping the crazymaking we pursue in staying with our addictions, being in denial, remaining apathetic, or trying to solve everything ourselves.

Within ecopsychology, this work is broadly thought of as waking up to the ecological crisis, though different writers have given it different names. Joanna Macy and her colleagues initially referred to it as "despair and empowerment work."[4] As we learned earlier, Mary E. Gomes and Allen D. Kanner label this as "challenging the lies of the false self."[5] Regardless what we call it, when we wake up, we begin to see that we have subscribed to a belief system that keeps us disconnected from the rest of the living world, instead concerned with trivial things such as our looks, our social media status, or the amount of stuff we own. Some of us even spiral into negative stories about how others have wronged us and continually inventory all the things we lack. In remaining so small and self-centered, we have forgone asking the bigger questions: What truly makes for a good life? How might we be of service to the greater good?

Waking up entails thinking more deeply about how our

actions leave damaging imprints on the planet—our accumulation of things, our fossil fuel consumption, our waste,
our silencing of nature. We begin to wonder what life would
be like if we stopped this madness and started connecting
to healthier, simpler ways of being. On the collective level,
we start witnessing what Macy and others call the "Great
Unraveling," describing the ways in which our current systems
start to break down under the accumulated weight of their
own greed and neglectfulness and where the human-caused
destruction of ecological systems becomes plain to see.[6]

Within social justice work, the term *decolonization* is often
employed to describe our waking up from systems of injus-
tice and reforming our mindsets and practices to no longer
be embedded within these faulty systems. Decolonization is
about disrupting our colonized minds and bodies; undoing
the damage of racism, sexism, ableism, homophobia, trans-
phobia, and all interlocking systems of oppression. When
we look at the analyses offered by the recovery movement,
ecopsychology, decolonization, and many other similar areas
of inquiry, a clear pattern appears. Each of these approaches
holds that our individual addictions and oppressions are part
and parcel of the same damaging systems of oppression—that
Earth and all her species are hurting from them, and we have
the power to disrupt this and to relearn and begin practicing
healthier ways of being.

For most people, the process of unraveling does not at first
feel like healing. To the contrary, it is disturbing to compre-
hend and often emotionally painful. (We will shortly look
deeper into this emotional pain and grief work.) Yet unraveling is essential as we begin to see and accept our individual

and collective issues and let the problematic stories that we have subscribed to for so long start to dissipate. This dissipation is critically important in order to make space for healthier stories. Unraveling our collective narcissism begins when we start seeing how we have been bred to be selfish, competitive, and often uncaring to other humans, nonhumans, and Earth. The process is challenging, but if we can stay with the work, we have a chance to create a more authentic, relational, and healthy world for all beings.

A couple of chapters back, we looked at how our belief systems, our worldviews, are constructed. If you recall, a worldview consists of a habit of mind and a resulting point of view. The habit of mind derives from all the external forces that condition our identities, including our politics, cultural and religious affiliations, and sense of morality. The resulting point of view is how we act out our habits of mind, such as the way we vote, whom we choose as friends and partners, what causes we contribute to, and what we see as right and wrong. The field of transformative learning offers a practice called a *disorienting dilemma* that I find incredibly helpful in working with people to unravel their worldviews.[7] I often create disorienting dilemma exercises to support folks who are waking up to our ecological and social crises and ready to shift their worldviews to cooperate, rather than compete with, nature and all beings.

A disorienting dilemma is essentially when we have an experience that perplexes us. It does not fit within our current worldview, so we experience what is labeled *cognitive dissonance*, essentially when our current experience clashes with our belief system. Typically, disorienting dilemmas are uncomfortable because we're confronted with something new that we either need to make work within our current belief system or expand our worldview to allow space to fit this new piece. While disorienting dilemmas are often formed from experiences in the present, I have found digging up *past* experiences that conflict with our current belief systems to be priceless in strengthening our processes of reflection and change. It strengthens our ability to unravel our worldview and create a more authentic one that serves the greatest whole. As we are working toward unraveling our individual and collective memes of narcissism, I thought it might be helpful to offer a disorienting dilemma practice here.

---

## EXERCISE

### A DISORIENTING DILEMMA, OUR NARCISSISTIC SELF

At the very beginning of this book, I shared a story from my childhood when I displayed narcissistic behavior: I did not want to fetch my hairbrush when my mother asked me to because I thought humans only had a limited number of movements in their lifetime and I did not want to waste mine. As silly as it sounds, at the core I was being selfish; I preferred that my mother waste her energy and I keep my own. In this exercise, I would like you to reflect on a moment in your life that you now see as being narcissistic. Remember that all of us are narcissistic at times, and this is actually healthy. To start, I would encourage you to take out your journal, if you have one, or a piece of paper and pen. (I like the physical quality of writing this way, but it is also okay if you use a computer.) Sit in a comfortable spot—if you have access to a peaceful space outside, this is often a great option.

Once you are ready, think of a time in your life when you acted in a way that you now see as narcissistic. Do not pick an acutely painful experience that may be accompanied by deep regret and a host of other emotions. Instead, pick a small instance, such as my silly brush story. Take a few minutes or so to write about this event, describing it in as much detail as you remember. If you can visualize the specifics of the experience (such as the setting, where you stood, etc.), all the better. Once you have this story down, please take a few additional minutes to reflect on the following questions:

- At the time your story occurred, how did you view yourself? What was your goal in life? What and whom did you care about?

Flashing forward to the present, take some additional time to answer the same questions:

- How do you currently view yourself? What is your goal in life? What and whom do you care about?

In comparing your first set of responses with your second, are they different? Do they indicate that you have changed? If so, create a list of words that signify the influences and experiences that may account for your change of view.

❀ ❀ ❀

I would like to build on our work here, employing this same process to examine the narcissistic ways we may have treated Earth. I am guessing that most of us can think of a time when we treated a nonhuman being or place narcissistically, acting with selfish disregard. I can model this with an example. I am ashamed to share that when I was seventeen years old and a senior in high school, I would blatantly litter. To be specific, I had my first car and, at the time, I smoked cigarettes. (Sorry, Mom.) I would drive around in my car smoking (and unnecessarily burning fossil fuels), and when the ashtray became overfull, I would stop at a deserted parking lot or similar low-key place, dump out the ashtray on the ground, get back into my car, and drive away. Yes, I know—this was unacceptable behavior that, in reflection, I regret and apologize for. At the time, I was very selfish, putting my needs above that of Earth. I was not thinking about anyone except myself, and while I had some shame around the fact that I smoked, I was shameless in my littering.

So there—I've given an example. Now I invite you to recall a story that you see as a time when you were narcissistic in your treatment of nature. Take a few minutes to write down the story, again visualizing as many of the specific details as you can remember. As before, please respond to the following questions:

- At the time your story occurred, how did you view yourself? What was your goal in life? What and whom did you care about? How did you view nature?

Flashing forward to the present, answer the same questions:

- How do you currently view yourself? What is your goal in life? What and whom do you care about? How do you view nature?

Once again, in comparing your first set of responses with your second, are they different? Have you changed? If so, create a list of words that signify the influences and experiences that may account for your change of view.

I extend my gratitude to you for engaging in this story-capturing and reflection process. While our stories may seem trivial, they actually hold significance for us and can be the smallest strands in unweaving a much bigger narrative.

---

## ATTENDING TO OUR EMOTIONS

*The truth is that things don't really get solved. They come together and they fall apart again. . . . The healing comes from letting there be room for all of this to happen: room for grief, for relief, for misery, for joy.*

—PEMA CHÖDRÖN[8]

I suspect, by your choice of reading, that you are not a stranger to your emotions. So much contemporary literature in psychology and spirituality focuses on the need to identify and work with our emotions. The work of healing our collective narcissism is no exception. Our Western and larger consumer cultures condition us to suppress our emotions—to see them as weak, irrational, and pointless. This is both tragic and ironic, since it is largely through manipulating our emotions that advertisers turn us again and again to the pursuit of our addictions—gaining power over others, accumulating money and things, or numbing ourselves with drugs, alcohol, technology, and codependent relationships. While there is a growing subset of our culture that fully embraces attending to our emotional selves, unfortunately so many within our societies are still avoiding them. We use an array of defense mechanisms in order to not experience our feelings. Emotions are scary, as they hold pain we have ignored for so long.

Yet by working with our deep emotions, we create incredible pathways toward healing.

I have been inspired by and draw from the works of so many practitioners on the power of attending to our emotions. Ecopsychology focuses heavily on the need to look at the pain we feel for Earth. I have mentioned the despair and empowerment work created by Joanna Macy and her colleagues. This work includes a strong focus on facing the emotional dimensions of the ecological crisis, and Macy developed it into a process called the "Work That Reconnects"—a kind of open-source and malleable set of views and practices that have inspired people around the world to practice with and build upon.[9] I was first introduced to Macy's work in the late 1990s. I was taking an ecopsychology class, and my teacher had recently returned from a workshop with Macy. She had a taped recording of some of the exercises and had us practice them. We initially starting walking slowly around the room; eventually we slowed down and connected with one another—staring into one another's eyes, witnessing one another. The sense of connection this work spurs is profound—embodied and emotional—and cannot be conveyed in words. As I started teaching my own ecopsychology courses, I regularly facilitated Macy's exercises. Within a few years, I met Joanna and have had the honor of knowing and working with her over the last couple of decades. A powerful example of her work is the Elm Dance, which Macy learned in Germany in the 1980s. She brought this dance to communities affected by the Chernobyl disaster. These communities were no longer able to spend time in nature, with the trees. By doing the Elm Dance, they were able to honor their relationship to the trees as well as their process of healing their communities.

In our last chapter, we looked at the three-step process Gomes and Kanner outline for working with a narcissistic personality and that extends to societal and ecological narcissism. If you recall, the second step focused upon working with "the pain and panic that arise as the false self crumbles"—the emotional fallout of waking up to our individual and collective narcissism.[10]

Attending to our emotions is part of and extends the process of unraveling, because as we reach acceptance that there is a problem, we begin to feel the deep emotions that have been resisted for so long. We honor all our emotions; there are no right or wrong ones. All our emotions are valid. Sadness, anger, apathy, fear, outrage, irritability, gloom, heartbrokenness, panic, hopelessness, suspicion, regret, overwhelm, and a host of other possible feelings are all welcome. The work is to allow ourselves to feel the emotions fully, within our minds, psyches, bodies, and hearts. Once we start feeling our emotions as connected to our individual and collective narcissism and we see how this has affected Earth and all beings, we can begin to change our behaviors. For example, as many of us become aware of our high levels of consumption and waste and how this results in damage to Earth, we often experience guilt, sadness, and even anger that we are immersed in systems that encourage waste and destruction. While we may initially feel overwhelmed, we may also become empowered to make small and large changes such as recycling, composting, biking or taking public transportation, shopping locally, and even downsizing our households.

Grieving is an incredibly important aspect of attending to our emotions. If you have ever lost a loved one—a person, pet, tree, or place you love—you can identify with the feeling of loss. Our grief is not linear; it comes in stages and waves that we learn to navigate through experience. Grief may never go away, but it can be held with love and honor. In general, people enculturated in Western societies do not grieve well due to our avoidance of emotions coupled with the busyness of our culture, which does not allot proper space and time to attend to our grief. And while it is common and acceptable to mourn a person or even a pet, grieving for the beings of nature or the loss of wild ecosystems is not a common practice.

In waking up to our individual and collective narcissism, part of the work is simply grieving the ways we have acted and allowing the associated emotions to surface. As we unpack and face our individual stories, the self-centeredness we may have held throughout our lives reveals itself. Have we thought of ourselves as more special than others? Have we focused too heavily on comparing and competing against our fellow humans? Have our needs continually taken precedence over those of others? Do we feel we deserve the good things in life because we are superior? Probably most of us have some measure of this type of thinking and, once again, this is normal—it is a conditioning we receive by our larger culture. Yet when we see and reflect on this, we may feel shame, sadness, and a host of other emotions associated with our conditionings, and we may need to grieve for the time we have lost in such foolish mindsets. And the very act of acquiescing to grief, with its loss of personal control, is a step toward a less self-centered way of being.

The ecologist Phyllis Windle stresses the importance for environmentalists to grieve, relating the process of ecological despair to mourning the loss of a beloved.[11] Windle illustrates that if one does not successfully grieve, they may either prolong their grief or repress it, causing additional problems. She writes that mourning for the ecological crisis differs from mourning a loved one in that, with the latter, the situation has at least a chance of closure through the finality of the death. Mourning the ecological crisis, by contrast, feels unending. As we learn of fresh losses of wild animal populations or whole species, new rounds of grieving get triggered. Even when we tap into the emotions and actively transform our behaviors toward Earth, we continue to witness her devastation. Hence, we need to develop additional forms of support to work with this grief. My hope is that the topics we cover within this chapter, including the guided meditation exercises and the resources I mention, can help with this.

Before we shift away from grief, there is another dynamic to ecological grief that I find fascinating. The psychoanalyst Joseph Dodds describes a Freudian phenomenon, *anticipatory mourning*, where a narcissist engages in a combination of avoiding and grieving a loss.[12] Here, the narcissist believes the loss is coming and shuts down emotionally while still feeling it at a subterranean level. If you recall, people with extreme narcissism have a pattern of shutting people out of their lives due to the damaged trust that developed during their early childhoods. The narcissist sustains a false self and a false reality that only allows in people and phenomena that reinforce their worldview. Those that do not are shunned, hence significant losses cannot truly be acknowledged. It is interesting to extend this idea of anticipatory mourning to how our individual and collective narcissism shuns the reality of our destruction of nature. Although on some level we all understand what is happening, we want to remain in a world where our habits of consumption are acceptable and where satisfying our individual needs remains our central focus. Knowing that the ecological crisis is real, unless we engage in a process of transformative personal and cultural change, we are left to partially mourn and partially shut out of our reality the losses caused by the crisis.

While scary, the work of attending to our emotions is paramount to the healing process. I love the saying "The only way out is through." To successfully navigate a difficulty, we have to get into it and encounter the terrain. In terms of our work here, this terrain is our emotional self. The deep work of actually feeling our emotions is precious, and when we learn to stay with our emotions, new capacities are revealed. As mentioned previously, Macy's "Work That Reconnects" provides wonderful experiential aspects that help us navigate the emotions that surface when working with the ecological crisis.

On a more personal level, when addressing dark and painful emotions, I find the work of the psychotherapist Miriam Greenspan and Pema Chödrön to be extremely supportive and insightful.[13] As Chödrön writes, "Working on ourselves and becoming more conscious about our own minds and emotions may be the only way for us to find solutions that address the welfare of all beings and the survival of the earth itself."[14]

When I became aware of the ecological crisis on a very deep level—understanding the many layers and connections between our larger history, economics, politics, and cultural practices—I plunged into a period of depression, anger, and sadness. The despair I felt seemed endless and unresolvable.

I had enough guidance from my studies and practices to stay with the emotions and allow myself to bottom out. What surfaced was a new stage of creativity, passion, and action that allowed me to actually work with these realities.

Many of my most profound meditation teachers have passed on an instruction called "touch and go" as a way to mindfully work with difficult emotions. The practice involves attending to difficult emotions as they arise, touching into them quite briefly, then letting one's attention to the emotion fall away. By doing so, we can experience our emotions without creating a heightened story about them or going too far past our current limits. I offer this practice here in a way that builds on our beginning exercise in chapter 1 as well as brings in your small story of narcissism we worked with earlier within this chapter.

---

### EXERCISE
#### TOUCH AND GO

Get into a comfortable, upright, seated position—whether on a chair, the floor, a cushion, even on the ground outside. Make your eyes soft, not staring at anything; or even close your eyes if this feels comfortable. Allow your body to be heavy—let your legs, sit bones (your seat), feet, and arms relax and be supported by the ground.

Imagine that you have deep roots forming from the base of your sit bones that plunge through the floor or ground below and deep into the earth. The roots move through any story levels, through the cement, eventually finding rich earth. Let your roots expand widely, feeling the sustenance of Earth. Allow your belly to be soft, and begin breathing deeply from your belly, generating heat. Let your inhales and exhales be deep, taking in cleansing air. Notice your posture and let your torso be upright. Elongate your neck and slightly tuck your chin.

Relax your mouth and jaw—you might even want to stretch out your mouth and stick out your tongue for a moment. Relax your face. Relax your eyes once more. Imagine the crown of your head has long branches reaching toward the sky that mirror your roots below. Notice any areas of pain or discomfort in your body and send a deep breath to these spaces.

Touch into your heart and notice if there is a dominant emotion that arises. Silently name this emotion and allow yourself to feel it fully in your body for a moment, breathing deeply in and out for a few breaths, letting this feeling permeate you. On your third out breath, release this emotion, as if a gentle, warm rain washes it away. Sit in silence for a minute or two, focusing on your breath.

Without bringing up the details, recall one feeling that surfaced when you reflected on your small story of narcissism toward another person earlier within this chapter. Silently name this emotion and allow yourself to feel it fully in your body for a moment, breathing deeply in and out for a few breaths, letting this feeling permeate you. On your third out breath, release this emotion, as if a gentle, warm rain washes it away. Sit in silence for a minute or two, focusing on your breath.

Once again, without going deeply into the story line, recall one feeling that surfaced when you reflected on your small story of narcissism toward Earth. Silently name this emotion and allow your-self to feel it fully in your body for a moment, breathing deeply in and out for a few breaths, letting this feeling permeate you. On your third out breath, release this emotion, as if a gentle, warm rain washes it away. Sit in silence for a minute or two, focusing on your breath.

Give gratitude to yourself for having the courage to feel your emotions. Know that you have countless allies from both the human and more-than-human natural world in this work. Sit in silence for a minute or two and gently come back into your surroundings.

---

## LOVE YOUR SELF

Given that we have spent a considerable amount of time in this book reflecting on the dangers of being fixated on a small, selfish sense of ego, it would be easy to start equating the ego with something bad and to constantly try to quell our ego needs. This is not actually the point of our work. While we want to dispel our individual and collective narcissism and the damage we are doing to all beings, loving our selves is extremely important for the work of healing. Loving the self in a nourishing manner goes beyond the ego but includes having a healthy sense of ego.

As mentioned earlier, the word *ego* in the context of narcissism tends to be equated with an overblown sense of self. Within a traditional psychological definition, however, the ego is merely a function of the mind that helps to establish our unique identity and what is real in the larger world while mediating between our conscious and unconscious realities. It organizes and holds our sense of reality in multifaceted ways, bringing our latent and hidden internal domains together with our perceptions and experiences of the external world. In general, the ego is a positive factor, and one we could not function without. A key difference between a narcissistic and a healthy ego is that the latter changes and develops over time. So what does it mean to practice loving our selves as we allow our egos to evolve?

The damaged ego has difficulties navigating our inner and outer worlds. On the foundational level, our minimal needs of nutritious food, clean water, clothing, housing, and health care must be intact. It may not be realistic for someone to do ego-repair work until their basic safety and physical needs are assured. Beyond the basics, much of the work of repairing the ego is restoring a sense of trust in other people as well as within ourselves. So many people in this world do not feel an authentic sense of purpose in life, nor do they feel themselves to be a part of a larger community. Having self-love is pivotal for the work of healing these psychological and social wounds. Luckily within Western society we have an abundance of therapists and counselors to attend to this dimension of the self. While an extreme narcissist often does not hold the self-awareness to recognize they have a problem, most people can engage such self-awareness and have the capacity to seek support. While I often critique mainstream psychology for focusing on a person's individual problems rather than our collective issues, I highly recommend that everyone goes through a certain amount of therapy with a licensed professional. Currently there is a vast array of both alternative and traditional therapies, so most folks can find a form that works for them. I do feel there is a connection between individual healing and collective healing—I do not believe one is a prerequisite for the other, yet they are both related and inseparable.

Authentically liking ourselves for who we are is essential for well-being, as is knowing that we are capable of self-actualization. Each of us needs to know we have the power to express our talents through using our inherent gifts and learned skills. While mainstream culture does not often tell us that we have a unique purpose in life, many wisdom traditions stress this message. Having a unique purpose is different from having a career pathway; it is a calling that is in service to something greater to the world. Having the opportunity and support to discover our purpose and build the skills necessary to carry it out brings freedom and capability. Feeling competent (as opposed to arrogant) is central to fostering a healthy self. When we feel this sense of competence, it is easier to truly like who we are and to trust our self. This sense of competence also supports our ability to create bigger visions for ourselves and for our communities. Likewise, it enhances our ability to experience healthy relationships in which we can cooperate well with others, authentically express ourselves, receive constructive feedback, and continually grow and change.

A major shift that needs to happen within our ego identities is to shed our addiction to individualism and recenter on relationships. The individual with damaged trust needs to attend to not only trusting the self but also trusting others—other humans and the more-than-human natural world. What with our Western, corporate, globalized civilization's fierce focus on individualism, so many of us have lost the art of connecting with and cooperating with others and often fear and mistrust one another. I like the poet John Donne's maxim, "No man is an island, entire of itself," for its clear recognition that each person is situated within a community—we are interconnected with other humans and nature.[15] While we often focus on needing to situate our individual health before engaging outward—the "put your own oxygen mask on first" phenomenon—the sustenance we need to grow into healthy beings is always in relationship to the larger system.

Think of a healthy plant. While on first glance it may appear as a separate being, it cannot survive without the larger ecosystem of soil, water, air, sunlight, nutrients, microbes, insects, and other plants. People are the same. The myth we hold in thinking we are isolated and completely self-determining is painful, and it becomes even more so when we believe we are in competition with one another. The two opening quotes of this chapter really speak to these ideals. While the twentieth-century Indian spiritual teacher Osho—also known as Rajneesh—is a problematic figure due to the cultlike atmosphere and antagonistic behavior that developed around him, I fully resonate with his statement about the oak and the bamboo trees not comparing themselves, which dispels the foolishness of the way humans are constantly ranking and competing against one another. The other quote, from Dr. Martin Luther King Jr., says something quite profound that we often overlook—our greatness is not determined by our individual accomplishments but by how we serve something greater. This is the measure of our full worth, and while our narcissistic culture keeps us focused on our individual successes, we will never find contentment and healing if we do not serve something greater.

## MINDFULNESS

*Mindfulness* is a very broad term that holds different meanings for different people. It has become overly popular in our culture, flooding the seminar circuits, apps, yoga aphorisms, and even the media. For our purposes, mindfulness is the practice of attending to the present moment, to what is at hand. Mindfulness, or more specifically mindful meditation, allows one to see clearly in the present moment, to see oneself within the present moment, and eventually to see larger circumstances and relationships in the present moment, which leads to becoming more skillful and hopefully more content and peaceful. When we attend to what is at hand, we become awake and aware. As our mindfulness skills increase, so does our capacity to serve all beings. One aspect I love about mindfulness practice is that when we find ourselves distraught and caught up in our thinking and negative emotions, often the antidote is to shift our focus and help others. In some of our upcoming sections, we will build on shifting outward and serving, but first we will shift to mindfulness.

The most basic and most advanced mindfulness practice is the ability to stay in one's present experience. Staying present is difficult for most of us, as we are conditioned to stay in the thinking mind—whether by thinking of something in the past or future or simply making up narratives or fantasies within our minds concerning just about anything. Staying with what is going on within our immediate experience is a skill we often forget. Although it is a natural ability, for most of us it takes some practice to revive and refine it.

For a person with extreme narcissism, remaining in the present is even more difficult, as they have created a story about themselves and others that they must continually keep up in order to protect themselves. Attending to the present moment could easily disrupt their story and, moreover, would require that they feel their emotions.

When we engage in mindfulness practice, our focus is on the immediate. Without the continual stories running in our minds, we may start to feel naked and exposed. When we let the story drop, what is left? What is our actual experience? Perhaps within the stillness of sitting meditation, we notice our breath; we inhabit and become aware of our bodily sensations; we notice the light, colors, sounds, and other sensations in our peripheral awareness. What is not in the immediate are the events that take place within the stories in our minds—the people and situations that may cause us stress, the ways we have failed others, any of the things we see as burdens, and even those things about which we are joyful and excited—these are carried within our thinking but are not our present experience. In meditation, we may notice we are thinking about these things and then remember the instruction to let them drop. What is left are the sensations we experience in the present moment. Mindfulness practice does not necessarily bring up joy—we may be experiencing sensations related to a short- or long-term illness, deep loss, depression, or other forms of suffering. Yet by staying with the experience of the present, we find an authentic ground of being and the courage to feel what is at hand and still find our center. We also start to notice how much of our suffering is related to the story of our suffering rather than the actual sensations themselves.

Within the collective narcissism of our society, we often feel that we need to be special and to have a continual audience to appreciate our uniqueness. When we become mindful to the present moment, our awareness may shift dramatically in noticing that we are now witnessing the present and we are just one of many beings within the larger landscape. We are simply ordinary and at the same time extraordinary, just like every other being. Many mindfulness traditions teach that our presence reflects the world around us, and through attentiveness we are both magnetized by our surroundings and are magnetizers. We begin to let our small sense of self unfold, opening to something much larger that still includes all of us.

I realize that I may be romanticizing mindfulness and meditation practice—these practices, like anything within our culture, can also be co-opted by our narcissistic traits. This is true across the scale, from formal institutions, which are often hierarchical and can foster harmful idolization of teachers as demigods; to competition between students; and even to within oneself. In the larger picture, it does not matter who can sit still for the longest with the most upright posture and the fewest thoughts. What matters is developing the abilities of awareness, perception, centering, and letting our stories about ourselves quell.

While it would seem that meditation would be a wonderful practice for a person with narcissistic personality disorder or extreme narcissism, this is not always the case. Some years back, when I was completing my meditation instructor training, I chose NPD as my research focus. As I began looking at the benefits of meditation for people with extreme levels of narcissism, I was surprised to find that meditation might not help someone with NPD at all. The psychoanalyst Pilar Jennings, for instance, has examined the scholarship of two different and groundbreaking researchers on the effectiveness of meditation for people with NPD.[16] The first, Heinz Kohut, focused on the undeveloped sense of self held by individuals with NPD. Kohut's approach was to work with "empathetic attunement," which "sought to facilitate more mature forms of narcissism, where a healthy, more reality-based investment in the self could be used to effectively interact with others."[17] In short, by having a therapist model empathy toward their narcissistic client, the narcissist begins to develop empathy toward their self. The second theorist, Otto Kernberg, did not support the use of empathy, claiming that since people with NPD suffered from feelings of envy and rage stemming from mistreatment by their early caregivers, empathy would not allow the "unprocessed rage" to surface and heal. Since meditation places such strong emphasis on empathy and compassion, it may be ineffectual for a person with NPD.

One of the defense tools a person with NPD employs is *splitting*, which means putting people and ideas into the categories of good and bad. Unable to integrate both the good and bad into their view of one person, someone with NPD is more likely to decide that a person is *either* good or bad.

> This use of splitting is applied to the self, whereby feelings of profound inferiority and unworthiness are not integrated into a more reality-based sense of one's talents and potential. Instead, the neurotic and pathological narcissist must protect feelings of grandiosity and omnipotent power through a chronic devaluation of others. A radar for the limitations and ineptitude of others, particularly for those who offer help and support, becomes a prominent defense.[18]

This use of splitting applies to spiritual practice as well. The typical meditator begins to become aware of their false self as practice brings up their habitual thought patterns. In contrast, someone with NPD may be unable to explore their self in practice and instead reinforces their sense of a grandiose self by gravitating to the godlike characteristics of figures such as the Buddha. The recommendation, therefore, is that the person with NPD also work with a therapist so they can address their early wounds and rebuild a healthy sense of self. The psychotherapist Mark Epstein, for example, highlights the dangers of meditation for a person with NPD by emphasizing how important it is that a meditator be able to confront the idealized self.[19]

> Meditation may ultimately be conceptualized as a vehicle for freeing an individual from their own narcissism, a liberation that is not complete until the experience of enlightenment. Until that point, the individual is subject to the pressures of their own narcissistic impulses. The experiences of meditation may even be recruited to satisfy those impulses, even as those experiences force a confrontation with narcissistic attachments.[20]

I know this is a lot of information to digest. Essentially what I want to communicate is that meditation may not work for an individual with NPD or extreme narcissism if they are unable to examine their constructs of self and attend to their early childhood wounds. This contemplative and analytical process requires a great deal of self-awareness and willingness to engage in work, and typically someone with extreme narcissism is not ready for this. In terms of our work here, I assume that most of us do not fall into the categories of extreme narcissism or NPD but rather, having been conditioned by our collective narcissism and having some sense of its detriments, are willing to look at our self-constructs and examine the pain we experience from our childhoods, the past in general, and the present. Meditation is an incredibly powerful practice that can assist us in reframing our individual and collective narcissism and learning to unravel our stories, feel our experiences, and develop increased compassion toward ourselves and other beings.

※ ※ ※

I highly appreciate the Zen teacher Ezra Bayda's "four basic reminders for practicing with emotional distress."[21] These are:

1. Awakening aspiration
2. Awakening curiosity
3. Awakening humor
4. Awakening loving-kindness

The four reminders apply to the general category of extreme states, and I think they translate to and are very useful for working with our individual and collective narcissism using meditation. To shift our narcissism to self-awareness and compassion, we must allow our false stories and fixations upon the self to dissipate. This involves feeling the underlying emotions that surface when we realize we are both ordinary and extraordinary, just like every being of Earth.

With the first reminder, "awakening aspiration," the meditator views the surfacing emotional disturbance as a "path to awakening." The suffering one experiences is real and, regardless of how it came to be, the sufferer can engage with it as a form of growth and potential healing. This engagement with mindfulness—a commitment to consciousness—can lead to a deep sense of wisdom, and the way to engage is to practice. It is through practice that we ground in what actually is, as opposed to how we want things to be or how things were in the past. It situates us into nowness and even, alarmingly, into the nowness of our distress when we surrender into our ordinariness and the resulting emotions that surface.

Bayda's second basic reminder, "awakening curiosity," is about getting into the actual experience of the present. We notice the sensations in our bodies, the quality and intensity of our emotions. It takes courage to feel difficult and extreme emotions without needing to move into a distraction or a defense mechanism, such as a different activity, an addiction, a denial, or an explaining story. Awakening curiosity is bringing our full attention to our suffering. When we apply this instruction to working with our narcissism, awakening curiosity brings us into awareness of our physical self without needing the attention of others. We can experience self-awareness and expression without needing an audience to admire us. This allows an authentic experience of the present to surface without needing to put on airs of display or worrying what others may think about us.

The third reminder is "awakening humor." It may sound a bit cruel to suggest for a person in extreme distress to find something funny about it. However, this is a different form of humor where one learns to put their suffering into a larger perspective. According to Bayda, it "serves as a reminder of the bigger view and helps generate compassion."[22] Our personal difficulties may feel awful and unfair, yet when we open to a wider view, we realize that there are others with much greater hardships. We live in a world where imprisonment, war, and genocide are widespread. We begin to see that everyone suffers. Yes, everyone suffers. This is far from humorous, yet we realize the irony of life. In shedding our narcissism, we see the foolishness of our being so self-consumed and shift our focus toward our usefulness to others.

Bayda phrases the final reminder as "awakening loving-kindness: allowing the spaciousness of the open heart to heal our deepest shame and darkest states of mind."[23] All of these practice reminders are challenging. It is difficult to accept one's suffering, feel it, and put it into a larger context. Bringing love and compassion back to one's self is perhaps the most difficult. When we come into contact with our authentic selves, our suffering, and our shame associated with our individual and collective narcissism, it is difficult to invoke love and healing. Yet this is precisely what we need—not love for the person we wish to project to others but love for the person we truly are, with all our faults, pain, and suffering. I often feed off feeling my pain. Sometimes it feels like one of the only authentic experiences in a world that is full of fake distractions. Money, glamour, success, television, drugs, alcohol, codependent relationships—these are so illusory; my pain feels real. It is letting go of the suffering and allowing love and compassion to flood in that is most difficult. Yet this is the path toward healing. We often attribute our challenges to flaws we must hold, yet so much of our suffering is not the result of our actions. Suffering simply comes with life.

As we move through these qualities of healing within this

chapter, you may feel burdened by the emotions that surface. As I mentioned before, the work of healing is not necessarily pleasant as it entails engaging our awareness, feelings, and actions regardless of their content. Yet most people who commit to this approach to life find that, over time, aspects of their experience that formerly seemed scary and unworkable now appear workable, lighter, sometimes even joyful. Meditation is an incredibly important tool in disrupting our self-involved story lines, coming back into awareness of our present experience, feeling our feelings, and acting with deeper compassion toward all beings.

Some years ago, I was at a meditation retreat that involved daily hours of silent sitting. While challenging, at some point I had an *aha!*—I realized that for me, sitting meditation was akin to what flowers do all day. I offer this exercise to inspire you to be comfortable with meditating within both your extraordinariness and ordinariness.

---

## EXERCISE
### THE SUNFLOWER

Find a comfortable sitting position and fully inhabit your body. Feel the heaviness of your sit bones, legs, and feet, and let your arms lie softly on your lap. Sit upright and allow your shoulders to melt down your back, your neck to elongate, your chin to tuck slightly, and your face and jaw to relax. Let your eyes be soft, not staring at anything. Deepen your breath, allowing your belly to lead your inhales and exhales. Breathe in silence for a minute or two.

Now imagine you have roots forming from your sit bones,

plunging deep into the earth and connecting you with soil and with all of life. These roots are the roots of a sunflower. Yes, imagine that you are a sunflower—once a dark seed, now sprouting and growing tall. You have strong roots, and your torso is a sturdy stalk of green matter, with shiny symmetrical leaves toward the top. You hold a beautiful crown—a friendly mass of newborn seeds, encircled with an abundance of brilliant, yellow petals. Yes, you are a sunflower: regal, bright, tall, radiating.

All day long, you shine your beauty, attend to the sun, provide refuge for birds and other beings, and simply attend to the present. Sit in silence for a few minutes, being this sunflower. Breathing in this moment, shift your sunflower vision outward and see that you are a regal, bright, tall, radiating sunflower amid a field of sunflowers equally regal, bright, radiating, and tall. Sit in silence for a few minutes breathing in and out, radiating, connecting.

---

## DEVELOPING YOUR ECOLOGICAL SELF

In chapter 4 we began examining the concept of the ecological self. We'll continue now to explore this possibility in more detail, as part of the transformative journey of healing from narcissism. While the term *ecological self* may be new to many folks, it is quite simple. To develop our ecological selves means to expand our self-capacities to identify not only with our small sense of self but to see and understand that our well-being is bound up with nature. In fact, it is the realization that we are nature.

If you recall, the field of ecopsychology centers upon how people of Western civilization (as well as societies immersed within corporate globalization) have essentially disconnected their identities from the rest of nature, spurring the ecological crisis and the collective trauma of people within these societies. As our collective narcissism is born out of this disconnection from nature and consequent identification with fierce individualism, consumerism, and a host of pathologies, a major aspect of the healing work is to reconnect with the more-than-human natural world. This is about recognizing our own sentience as beings of nature as well as developing our compassion toward nature.

On the basic level, developing our ecological selves is about feeling at home within nature—learning to trust nature, building our abilities to survive within the natural world, and feeling a sense of wonder and awe when immersed in nature. So many people in our society fear nature—she is a stranger to them, and often a dangerous one. The field of ecotherapy has some wonderful practices for reconnecting with nature that are gentle and fulfilling. Yet we do not necessarily need to pay someone to teach us how to connect with nature. Nature is everywhere—in wilderness areas, yes, but also within a city park. Nature is the air that we breathe, rain and snow, sunlight, soil, insects, animals, and all other beings of Earth, including other humans. Simply spending time with nature and recognizing nature build this awareness.

Developing a personal relationship with nature is precious work. For some of us, it is the simple appreciation of a tree or the summer rain. For others it becomes more transpersonal, recognizing that all of life is connected and that nature itself is bigger than the human-centered world.

Developing our ecological selves is also about serving something greater. While ecotherapy and other therapeutic practices in nature are very important, they tend to use a lens that focuses more on what nature can do for us rather than what we can do for Earth. The various aspects of healing our collective narcissism—unraveling our story lines, feeling our emotions, grieving, attending to the present moment, and connecting with nature—help us develop into healthy, mature adults who are willing to attend to the needs of the greater good, to all living beings. To do this work of healing, we must attend to the reality of the ecological crises and our role within them. There is something profound when we begin to develop a reciprocal relationship with nature, realizing that we affect and are affected by the living systems of Earth. We realize that the beings of Earth and Earth herself are alive. This realization opens up both metaphoric and literal conversations with nature—we recognize a larger consciousness within nature that links us to a deeper experience of reality. For many of us, when we develop our compassion toward Earth, we see that this is reciprocated and that nature often serves as a guide or helper to us.

In terms of shedding our collective narcissism, when we develop our ecological selves and open up to the larger consciousness of nature, we enlarge our world, our reality. We step out of a story line that is always authored by our selves and allow other entities to be a part of and actually lead the story. This process takes a great deal of trust, so to engage it, we need to start small and slowly build our relationship with nature. As we immerse in the natural world, we also may see that we are just a very small drop within a vast expanse of life. I will not offer a formal exercise for developing our ecological self, as so many of the exercises I have already introduced do so. I would recommend that you simply find a peaceful place outside and repeat the first exercise we did, this time letting yourself sit silently in nature at the end of the practice and noticing what happens.

## BUILDING COMPASSION TOWARD OTHERS

Throughout this book, we have referred to the primary traits of a narcissist—a grandiose sense of self, arrogance, very low empathy for others, shamelessness, hypersensitivity to critique (fragile ego), and an overall constant need to feel more special than others. All these traits demonstrate that, at its core, extreme narcissism means having difficulty feeling compassion toward other beings. A person with NPD may not be self-aware of their lack of compassion, yet it is evident to those around them. This lack of awareness is due to the damaged trust they accrued in early childhood and their perpetual need to create a putatively safe, false reality that is centered around their self. If you have interacted with a narcissist, you have probably noticed these traits: they always redirect the conversation back to themselves; often ignore or quickly dismiss things you bring up about yourself; and they become annoyed, even angry, and may even disappear for some time if you need assistance from them. The narcissist is threatened when the center of attention shifts away from them, and it is very challenging for them to extend their awareness to the needs of others.

Translating this dynamic to our collective narcissism, it seems more and more people have underdeveloped social skills—not only in the typical sense of that term but also in the deep sense of knowing how to cultivate meaningful human connection. With our society's heavy focus on individualism, the art of connecting with and serving the larger community is often lost. There is a trend, exacerbated by social media, to surround ourselves with people who reflect our values and to not engage with difference. And even with folks we choose to interact with, there is often an attitude of *me first*. The political scientist Robert Putnam refers to the term *social capital*—essentially our investment in relationships—and illustrates the decline of community that has occurred over a series of decades dating to the post–World War II era.[24] This decline paralleled and directly related to the growth of the industrialized, corporate globalized world. It marked a shift away from investing in resources within one's community— the local economy, yes, but also relationships, cultural diversity, and caring for nature.[25] Within the collective narcissism of our society, we have moved away from the importance of social ties, lessening our stock of social capital that includes qualities such as "generosity," "trustworthiness," and "mutual obligation and responsibility."[26] Globalization has essentially stripped from people the resources of connection and community, keeping us alienated, competitive, and often lonely.

In a capitalistic, corporate globalized world, relationships are often transactional rather than altruistic. Individuals tend to be opportunistic, only entering into relationships when there is something to be gained from the other person or group. Does this relationship elevate my status and finances? Will this person do and give me things that I desire? There seems to be a lack of understanding that giving to others, being of service, is something that increases our well-being, regardless of what someone does for us. Of course, we want reciprocity in our relationships, and we certainly do not want to be in relationships where people take from us without caring for our needs. Yet I find that, in general, caring and support are not, and need not be, strictly equitable within one-to-one relationships. Rather, the caring and support we need come from a much larger pool when we open up to this possibility. Ironically, in a capitalistic, individualist society, love is viewed as a scarce commodity that is often only provided by one's most intimate relationship, such as with a partner, child, or parent. We omit the possibility that we can receive love from a larger circle—from friends, community members, even strangers. Relating this to compassion and narcissism, I appreciate the wisdom of the clinical psychologist and Jungian analyst Dr. Eve Maram, who connects the missing component that bridges narcissism and compassion—*eros*.

> In Jungian terms, the principle of eros is a form of love (that Greeks personified as the god of love, Eros), involving psychic relatedness and the spontaneous, deep-rooted urge to connect. Eros conveys tremendous healing potential, evident in the natural human urge for wholeness or the satisfaction of relating with others on a deeply feeling level.[27]

Just as with developing our healthy egos as well as our ecological selves, building our compassion toward other people requires restoring our trust in the world and one another, which requires working on our skills to connect and relate. When we close down our worldviews to protect ourselves, we often shut down our emotions, senses, and forms of expression, thus diminishing our capacity to attend to our own needs and those of others. We miss the social cues of looking into someone's eyes, smiling at one another, sensing someone's mood, asking about someone's story and needs, and responding.

In one of his final insights looking at the possible connection between eros and narcissism and linking them as a pathway toward evolutionary development, Theodore Roszak, the founder of ecopsychology, wrote, "It may be that . . . narcissism is the compensatory balance our threatened planet needs if it is to restrain the excesses of industrial growth."[28] How could he possibly make an argument such as that? Essentially Roszak was drawing on the Freudian concept of *primary narcissism*—the fixation on pleasure we first experience as a child. He applied this idea to our current narcissism, arguing that the basic human drive toward pleasure might serve as a way to halt our unending economic growth with its attendant ecological devastation. Making sense of this argument requires opening to the possibility that such a drive could be satisfied in healthier and more sustainable ways than through our current compulsion to acquire new things and experiences. Roszak's idea, for instance, pairs well with the work of the philosopher Herbert Marcuse, who championed the idea of the *Great Refusal*—a countermovement against the constant labor and rationality of the industrial age, emphasizing instead the possibility of shifting back toward the sensory delights of childhood. This also relates to the longing for the eros found in deep connection. This insight is too complex to turn toward here, but worth noting. And we certainly need to drop into our sensory experiences as part of the work of shedding our narcissism and healing ourselves and Earth.

When we reawaken to our inherent capacities to experience our bodies, hearts, and minds within the present moment and the company of nature in our present space, we begin a path of richness that surpasses material longings. We begin to come home.

As we build our compassion, we must learn to stretch across positionalities such as race, class, gender, sexual expression, and politics that have too often been framed as either-or binaries. As you may recall, the narcissist quickly posits people in good and bad camps, shunning the bad and surrounding themselves with what they perceive as good or right. We also do this within our collective narcissism, identifying people we see as having the right types of values—those that mirror our own—and shunning those who do not. This is very evident in our political divides and is quite manifest in issues of race. In a previous chapter, we witnessed the blatant lack of compassion that was birthed from colonization, specifically in the US, surrounding the oppression toward First Nations peoples as well as enslaved Africans. Dehumanization is a founding trait within colonized nations, and hence we have tremendous work to do in unraveling this and learning to be compassionate toward one another. We also looked at how this low level of empathy has directly translated into the ways we treat Earth.

Within our last chapter, we examined a number of framings of self—the ecological self, the interdependent self as seen in the Buddhist teaching of the skandhas, the pluralistic and spiritual Self with a capital *S*. I would like to introduce one more such framing that is quite helpful in building our individual and collective compassion. The *multicultural self* is a concept coined by my dear mentor Carl C. Anthony,[29] and

I like to pair it with additional framings when working with expanding worldviews around social and ecological issues.

In essence, the multicultural self is about learning the stories of the people around you. What starts with people nearby can then extend to the wider community and beyond, developing into an ongoing genuine curiosity about other people's stories and cultures. It is about learning about people one might consider the "other," recognizing their humanity, and building empathy between one another. When we build this type of compassion, we greatly reduce our fear and isolation and step out of our individual, often narcissistic selves. When that happens, we truly open the door to starting to serve the greater good.

I first heard one of my all-time favorite examples of a multicultural self on the New York Public Radio show *Radio Lab*.[30] The story is about a small, conservative town in Oregon that ends up electing a transgender mayor, Stu Rasmussen, in 2009. At heart, folks overlooked their prejudices and elected Stu because everyone knew him. The climax of the story is how the community even defends the mayor from hostile people from neighboring communities. It is a perfect example of people dropping their preconceived biases and replacing them with compassionate action.

## GRACE

*You only need a heart full of grace, a soul generated by love.*
—**MARTIN LUTHER KING JR.**[31]

*People laugh up their sleeves at anything that defies*
*the industrial explanation of our lives, anything that is*

*spiritual. But these experiences are grace. Interacting with nonhumans doesn't have anything to do with gathering information; it has to do with being blessed. And wanting to be blessed. It has to do with that intersection of communication and communion.*

—DERRICK JENSEN[32]

Within our last chapter we also engaged many concepts that ventured into a transpersonal reality, one that includes and goes beyond the physical plane of existence bringing in many unseen and mysterious dimensions to our experience of life. The transpersonal falls into the realms of spirituality and nonordinary states of awareness. These experiences cannot be explained or comprehended by the rational, thinking mind; rather, they are perceived by the domains of our sensory awareness, our feelings, our dream world, and the unconscious. Often grace appears as the experience of the very extraordinary within the ordinary. It can arise when we engage in very simple activities and bring our full attention to them—sipping a cup of tea, feeling the wind brush up against us, making eye contact with a wild being. It is a moment when we encounter the stillness of our mind amid contact with something greater. It is a moment when we allow our defenses to drop and something extraordinary enters.

As we unravel the damage of corporate globalization, colonization, and so many other forms of oppression, many of us fear believing in anything that may further condition us, especially religion and spirituality. Religion in particular has been used within systems of oppression to silence earth-based peoples, women, people of color, and so many forms of identity and free expression. Yet our ability to tap into the transpersonal domain, to open to grace, is perhaps the most important aspect of healing our collective narcissism.

The narcissist is threatened by the transpersonal as it requires opening up to something outside of their false self, their constructed reality. It requires acknowledging something they are not in control of and that is much vaster than they are. I appreciate the Jungian analyst Nancy Furlotti's words about the disdain the narcissist has for spirituality: "Stepping into relationship, which means giving over control to something more powerful, . . . is exactly what the narcissist cannot allow to happen."[33]

Paralleling such individual narcissists, our collectively narcissistic society believes deeply in the power of the individual and that we each are self-authoring and independent. This individualistic view requires not subscribing to something that is more powerful and out of our control. Fixated on our small egos, we have become addicted to being in control. As the writer Laurence Boldt aptly claims, "The development of the ego is also recognized as a loss. It is represented poetically as the original fall from grace."[34] This fall from grace is part of our individual and collective stories—the damaged trust many experienced in early childhood as well as our separation from nature, including one another. Stepping into grace is about reclaiming our trust in the world, fully understanding that we can surrender to something greater. This relates to the second step in recovery, where after admitting we have a problem, we turn it over to a higher power. For some this is God, for others this is nature, for others the transpersonal. Whatever name one uses, it is the process of grace, of once again coming home to this world with trust and allowing guidance from sources beyond the self.

When we allow our sense of self, grounded in the present moment, to expand from the small ego to these larger sources—our emotional lives, nature, community, the transpersonal—healing begins. We enter into the sacredness of life and can come out of our narcissistic worlds to a space of communion. This is not necessarily always a pleasant space, but it is authentic. It is the space in which we stand our best chance to develop the maturity we need to live in harmony with one another, including all beings of Earth. We come into acceptance that we do not know everything, we are not always in control, we may not be the best but we can be our greatest—we are truly ordinary and extraordinary.

# NOTES

**PREFACE**

1. Tyson Yunkaporta, *Sand Talk: How Indigenous Thinking Can Save the World* (New York: HarperOne, 2020), 17.
2. Scott Barry Kaufman, "The Opposite of Toxic Positivity," *The Atlantic*, August 18, 2021, https://www.theatlantic.com/family/archive/2021/08/tragic-optimism-opposite-toxic-positivity/619786/.

**CHAPTER 1: A NEW UNDERSTANDING OF NARCISSISM**

1. Jean M. Twenge and W. Keith Campbell, *The Narcissism Epidemic: Living in the Age of Entitlement* (New York: Harper Perennial, 2009).
2. Craig Malkin, *Rethinking Narcissism: The Secret to Recognizing and Coping with Narcissists* (New York: Harper Perennial, 2015), 10–12.
3. JH Simon, *How to Kill a Narcissist: Debunking the Myth of Narcissism and Recovering from Narcissistic Abuse* (self-pub., 2016), 66.
4. Twenge and Campbell, *Narcissism Epidemic*, 56.
5. Allen D. Kanner and Mary E. Gomes, "The All-Consuming Self," in *Ecopsychology: Restoring the Earth, Healing the Mind*, ed. Theodore Roszak, Mary E. Gomes, and Allen D. Kanner (San Francisco: Sierra Books), 79.

**CHAPTER 2: FRAMING NARCISSISM**

1. Susan M. Koger and Deborah Du Nann Winter, *The Psychology of Environmental Problems: Psychology for Sustainability* (New York: Psychology Press, 2010), 41–45.

2. Koger and Winter, *Psychology of Environmental Problems*, 45.

3. Donald W. Winnicott, "Ego Distortion in Terms of True and False Self," in *The Maturational Processes and the Facilitating Environment: Studies in the Theory of Emotional Development*, ed. Donald W. Winnicott (London: Karnac Books, 1960), 140–52.

4. Nancy Furlotti, "Narcissism in the Home," in *A Clear and Present Danger: Narcissism in the Era of Donald Trump*, ed. Leonard Cruz and Steve Buser (Asheville, NC: Chiron Publications, 2016), 151–52.

5. Joe Willie Namath, *I Can't Wait Until Tomorrow . . . 'Cause I Get Better Looking Every Day* (New York: Random House, 1969).

6. JH Simon, *How to Kill a Narcissist: Debunking the Myth of Narcissism and Recovering from Narcissistic Abuse* (self-pub., 2016), 43.

7. Ramani S. Durvasula, *"Don't You Know Who I Am?": How to Stay Sane in an Era of Narcissism, Entitlement, and Incivility* (New York: Post Hill Press, 2019), 103.

8. Durvasula, *"Don't You Know Who I Am?"* 104.

9. *The Mean World Syndrome: Media Violence & the Cultivation of Fear*, written and directed by Jeremy Earp (Northampton, MA: Media Education Foundation, 2010), film transcript, https://www.mediaed.org/transcripts/Mean-World-Syndrome-Transcript.pdf.

10. Christopher Lasch, *The Culture of Narcissism: American Life in an Age of Diminishing Expectations* (New York: W. W. Norton, 1979), 13.

11. Audre Lorde, *A Burst of Light: Essays* (Ithaca, NY: Firebrand Books, 1988), 130.

12. Allen D. Kanner and Mary E. Gomes, "The All Consuming Self," in *Ecopsychology: Restoring the Earth, Healing the Mind*, ed. Theodore Roszak, Mary E. Gomes, and Allen D. Kanner (San Francisco: Sierra Books, 1995), 77–91.

13. This argument is developed at length in Jean M. Twenge and W. Keith Campbell, *The Narcissism Epidemic: Living in the Age of Entitlement* (New York: Harper Perennial, 2009).

14. Durvasula, *"Don't You Know Who I Am?"* 36.

15. Durvasula, *"Don't You Know Who I Am?"* 63.

16. Steve Buser "The Trump Complex, the John Wayne Archetype and

States of National Possession," in *A Clear and Present Danger: Narcissism in the Era of Donald Trump*, ed. Leonard Cruz and Steve Buser (Asheville, NC: Chiron Publications, 2016), 14.

## CHAPTER 3: ECOLOGICAL CRISIS AND NARCISSISTIC PERSONALITY DISORDER

1. Jack Mezirow, "Transformative Learning: Theory to Practice," in *Transformative Learning in Action: Insights from Practice*, ed. Patricia Cranton (Cummings, GA: Jossey-Bass, 1997), 5–12.

2. Chellis Glendinning, *My Name Is Chellis & I'm in Recovery from Western Civilization* (Boston: Shambhala Publications, 2007).

3. Glendinning, *My Name Is Chellis*, 69–70.

4. *The Burning Times*, directed by Donna Read, in Women and Spirituality: The Goddess Trilogy (Montreal: National Film Board of Canada, 1990), video recording; Silvia Federici, *Caliban and the Witch: Women, the Body and Primitive Accumulation* (New York: Autonomedia, 2004).

5. Starhawk, *The Earth Path: Grounding Your Spirit in the Rhythms of Nature* (San Francisco: HarperSanFrancisco, 2004).

6. Susan M. Koger and Deborah Du Nann Winter, *The Psychology of Environmental Problems: Psychology for Sustainability* (New York: Psychology Press, 2010), 41–42.

7. Richard Louv, *Last Child in the Woods: Saving Our Children from Nature-Deficit Disorder* (Chapel Hill, NC: Algonquin Books, 2008).

8. Glendinning, *My Name Is Chellis*, 20–21.

9. Allen D. Kanner and Mary E. Gomes, "The All-Consuming Self," in *Ecopsychology: Restoring the Earth, Healing the Mind*, ed. Theodore Roszak, Mary E. Gomes, and Allen D. Kanner (San Francisco: Sierra Books, 1995), 77–91.

10. Paul Shepard, "Nature and Madness," in *Ecopsychology: Restoring the Earth, Healing the Mind*, ed. Theodore Roszak, Mary E. Gomes, and Allen D. Kanner (San Francisco: Sierra Books, 1995), 21–40.

11. Deane Curtin, "One World Under God," in *Environmental Ethics for a Postcolonial World* (Boulder, CO: Rowman & Littlefield Publishers, 2005), 1–25.

12. Joanna Macy and Molly Young Brown, *Coming Back to Life: Practices to Reconnect Our Lives, Our World* (Gabriola Island, BC: New Society Publishers, 1998).

13. Jeanine M. Canty, "Walking Between Worlds: Holding Multiple Worldviews as a Key for Ecological Transformation," *International Journal of Transpersonal Studies* 33, no. (2014): 15–26.

14. Macy and Brown, *Coming Back to Life*, 34–37.

15. Carl C. Anthony, "Ecopsychology and the Deconstruction of Whiteness," in *Ecopsychology: Restoring the Earth, Healing the Mind*, ed. Theodore Roszak, Mary E. Gomes, and Allen D. Kanner (San Francisco: Sierra Books), 263–78.

16. Donald E. Collins, "Racism and Narcissism: America's Original Sin," *Aljazeera*, August 10, 2019.

17. Jean M. Twenge and W. Keith Campbell, *The Narcissism Epidemic: Living in the Age of Entitlement* (New York: Atria, 2009), 152.

18. Robin DiAngelo, "White Fragility," *International Journal of Critical Pedagogy* 3, no. 3 (2011): 54–70.

19. Carl C. Bell, "Racism: A Symptom of the Narcissistic Personality," *Journal of the National Medical Association* 72, no. 7 (1980): 661–65.

20. Ramani S. Durvasula, *"Don't You Know Who I Am?" How to Stay Sane in an Era of Narcissism, Entitlement, and Incivility* (New York: Post Hill Press, 2019), 72.

21. Tom Singer, "Trump and the American Selfie: Archetypal Defenses of the Group Spirit," in *A Clear and Present Danger: Narcissism in the Era of Donald Trump*, ed. Leonard Cruz and Steve Buser (Asheville, NC: Chiron Publications, 2016), 42.

22. Nancy Furlotti, "Narcissism in Our Collective Home, Our American Culture," in *A Clear and Present Danger: Narcissism in the Era of Donald Trump*, ed. Leonard Cruz and Steve Buser (Asheville, NC: Chiron Publications, 2016), 203.

CHAPTER 4: THE FALSE SELF

1. Allen D. Kanner and Mary E. Gomes, "The All Consuming Self," in *Ecopsychology: Restoring the Earth, Healing the Mind*, ed. Theodore

Roszak, Mary E. Gomes, and Allen D. Kanner (San Francisco: Sierra Books, 1995), 77–91.

2. Derrick Jensen, *A Language Older than Words* (White River Junction, VT: Chelsea Green Publishing, 2004), ix.

3. Arne Naess, "Self-Realization: An Ecological Approach to Being in the World," in *Deep Ecology for the 21st Century: Readings on the Philosophy and Practice of the New Environmentalism*, ed. George Sessions (Boston: Shambhala Publications, 1995), 225–39.

4. Joanna Macy, *World as Lover, World as Self: Courage for Global Justice and Ecological Renewal* (Berkeley, CA: Parallax Press, 2007), 148.

5. Pema Chödrön, *Taking the Leap: Freeing Ourselves from Old Habits and Fears* (Boston: Shambhala Publications, 2010), 16.

6. Chödrön, *Taking the Leap*, 21–22.

7. Chödrön, *Taking the Leap*, 4.

8. Tsultrim Allione, *Feeding Your Demons: Ancient Wisdom to Healing Inner Conflict* (New York: Little, Brown, 2008), 15–16.

9. James Hillman, *The Soul's Code: In Search of Character and Calling* (New York: Warner Books, 1996), 8.

10. Ralph Metzner, *The Unfolding Self: Varieties of Transformative Experience* (Ross, CA: Pioneer Imprints, 2010), 133.

11. Allione, *Feeding Your Demons*, 15–16.

12. Allione, *Feeding Your Demons*, 43.

## CHAPTER 5: TOWARD HEALING SELF AND PLANET

1. Martin Luther King Jr., "The Drum Major Instinct" (sermon, Ebenezer Baptist Church, Atlanta, GA, February 4, 1968).

2. Osho, *Osho Zen Tarot: The Transcendental Game of Zen* (New York: St. Martin's Press, 1994), 127.

3. Belvie Rooks, "Healing the Wounds of Slavery and the Planet," in *Ecological and Social Healing: Multicultural Women's Voices*, ed. Jeanine M. Canty (New York: Routledge, 2017), 199.

4. Joanna Macy and Molly Young Brown, *Coming Back to Life: Practices to Reconnect Our Lives, Our World* (Gabriola Island, BC: New Society Publishers, 1998), 5.

5. Allen D. Kanner and Mary E. Gomes, "The All-Consuming Self," in *Ecopsychology: Restoring the Earth, Healing the Mind*, ed. Theodore Roszak, Mary E. Gomes, and Allen D. Kanner (San Francisco: Sierra Books, 1995), 77–91.

6. Joanna Macy and Chris Johnstone, *Active Hope: How to Face the Mess We're In without Going Crazy* (Novato, CA: New World Library, 2012).

7. Jeanine M. Canty, "Seeing Clearly through Cracked Lenses," in *Ecological and Social Healing: Multicultural Women's Voices*, ed. Jeanine M. Canty (New York: Routledge, 2017), 23–44.

8. Pema Chödrön, *When Things Fall Apart: Heart Advice for Difficult Times* (Boston: Shambhala Publications, 1997), 8.

9. Stephanie Kaza, ed., *A Wild Love for the World: Joanna Macy and the Work of Our Time* (Boulder, CO: Shambhala Publications, 2021).

10. Kanner and Gomes, "All-Consuming Self," 88.

11. Phyllis Windle, "The Ecology of Grief," in *Ecopsychology: Restoring the Earth, Healing the Mind*, ed. Theodore Roszak, Mary E. Gomes, and Allen D. Kanner (San Francisco: Sierra Books), 136–48.

12. Joseph Dodds, *Psychology and Ecology at the Edge of Chaos* (New York: Routledge, 2011).

13. Miriam Greenspan, *Healing through Dark Emotions: The Wisdom of Grief, Fear, and Despair* (Boston: Shambhala Publications, 2003); Pema Chödrön, *When Things Fall Apart: Heart Advice for Difficult Times* (Boston: Shambhala Publications, 1997).

14. Pema Chödrön, *Taking the Leap: Freeing Ourselves from Old Habits and Fears* (Boston: Shambhala Publications, 2010), 1.

15. John Donne, "No Man Is an Island," in *Devotions Upon Emergent Occasions* (London: 1624).

16. Pilar Jennings, "East of Ego: The Intersection of Narcissistic Personality and Buddhist Practice," *Journal of Religion and Health* 46, no. 1 (March 2007): 3–18.

17. Jennings, "East of Ego," 6.

18. Jennings, "East of Ego," 8.

19. Mark Epstein, "Meditative Transformations of Narcissism," *Journal of Transpersonal Psychology* 18, no. 2 (1986): 143–58.

20. Epstein, "Meditative Transformations of Narcissism," 155.

21. Ezra Bayda, *Being Zen: Bringing Meditation to Life* (Boulder, CO: Shambhala Publications, 2002), 93.

22. Bayda, *Being Zen*, 91.

23. Bayda, *Being Zen*, 93.

24. Robert. D. Putnam, "Thinking about Social Change in America," in *Bowling Alone: The Collapse and Revival of American Community* (New York: Simon and Schuster, 2000), 15–28.

25. Jeanine M. Canty, "The Ties that Bind: An Earth-Based Story of Home," in *Globalism and Localization: Emergent Approaches to Ecological and Social Crises* (New York: Routledge, 2019), 34–53.

26. Putnam, "Thinking about Social Change in America," 20–21.

27. Eve Maram, "Narcissism and Social Media: Eros Held Hostage," in *A Clear and Present Danger: Narcissism in the Era of Donald Trump*, ed. Leonard Cruz and Steve Buser (Asheville, NC: Chiron Publications, 2016), 166.

28. Theodore Roszak, *Voice of the Earth: An Exploration of Ecopsychology* (Grand Rapids, MI: Phanes Press, 2001), 265.

29. Carl C. Anthony, "Ecopsychology and the Deconstruction of Whiteness," in *Ecopsychology: Restoring the Earth, Healing the Mind*, ed. Theodore Roszak, Mary E. Gomes, and Allen D. Kanner (San Francisco: Sierra Books), 263–78.

30. Aaron Scott, "The New Stu," *Radio Lab*, October 19, 2009, https://www.wnycstudios.org/podcasts/radiolab/segments/91695-new-stu.

31. King, "The Drum Major Instinct."

32. Derrick Jensen, *A Language Older Than Words* (White River Junction, VT: Chelsea Green Publishing, 2000), 69.

33. Nancy Furlotti, "Narcissism in Our Collective Home, Our American Culture," in *A Clear and Present Danger: Narcissism in the Era of Donald Trump*, ed. Leonard Cruz and Steve Buser (Asheville, NC: Chiron Publications, 2016), 203.

34. Laurence G. Boldt, *The Tao of Abundance: Eight Ancient Principles for Abundant Living* (New York: Penguin Putnam, 1999), 29.

# RESOURCES FOR
# FURTHER READING

Allione, Tsultrim. *Feeding Your Demons: Ancient Wisdom for Resolving Inner Conflict*. New York: Little, Brown, 2008.

Behary, Wendy T. *Disarming the Narcissist: Surviving and Thriving with the Self-Absorbed*. Oakland, CA: New Harbinger Publications, 2013.

Campbell, W. Keith, with Carolyn Crist. *The New Science of Narcissism: Understanding One of the Greatest Psychological Challenges of Our Time—and What You Can Do about It*. Boulder, CO: Sounds True, 2020.

Canty, Jeanine M. "Walking Between Worlds: Holding Multiple Worldviews as a Key for Ecological Transformation." *International Journal of Transpersonal Studies* 33, no. 1(2014): 15–26.

Chödrön, Pema. *Taking the Leap: Freeing Ourselves from Old Habits and Fears*. Boston: Shambhala Publications, 2010.

Chödrön, Pema. *When Things Fall Apart: Heart Advice for Difficult Times*. Boston: Shambhala Publications, 1997.

Cruz, Leonard, and Steven Buser, eds. *A Clear and Present Danger: Narcissism in the Era of Donald Trump*. Asheville, NC: Chiron Publications, 2016.

Dodds, Joseph. *Psychology and Ecology at the Edge of Chaos*. New York: Routledge, 2011.

Durvasula, Ramani S. *"Don't You Know Who I Am?" How to Stay Sane in an Era of Narcissism, Entitlement, and Incivility*. New York: Post Hill Press, 2019.

Glendinning, Chellis. *My Name Is Chellis & I'm in Recovery from Western Civilization*. Boston: Shambhala Publications, 2007.

Greenspan, Miriam. *Healing through Dark Emotions: The Wisdom of Grief, Fear, and Despair*. Boston: Shambhala Publications, 2003.

Kaza, Stephanie, ed. *A Wild Love for the World: Joanna Macy and the Work of Our Time*. Boulder, CO: Shambhala Publications, 2021.

Koger, Susan. M., and Deborah Du Nann Winter. *The Psychology of Environmental Problems: Psychology for Sustainability*. New York: Psychology Press, 2010.

Lasch, Christopher. *The Culture of Narcissism: American Life in an Age of Diminishing Expectations*. New York: W. W. Norton, 1979.

Louv, Richard. *Last Child in the Woods: Saving Our Children from Nature-Deficit Disorder*. Chapel Hill, NC: Algonquin Books, 2005.

Loy, David. R. *EcoDharma: Buddhist Teachings for the Ecological Crisis*. Somerville, MA: Wisdom Publications, 2018.

Macy, Joanna. *World as Lover, World as Self: Courage for Global Justice and Ecological Renewal*. Berkeley, CA: Parallax Press, 2007.

Macy, Joanna, and Molly Young Brown. *Coming Back to Life: Practices to Reconnect Our Lives, Our World*. Gabriola Island, BC: New Society Publishers, 1998.

Macy, Joanna, and Chris Johnstone. *Active Hope: How to Face the Mess We're In without Going Crazy*. Novato, CA: New World Library, 2012.

Malkin, Craig. *Rethinking Narcissism: The Secret to Recognizing and Coping with Narcissists*. New York: HarperCollins, 2016.

Metzner, Ralph. *The Unfolding Self: Varieties of Transformative Experience*. Ross, CA: Pioneer Imprints, 2010.

Naess, Arne. "Self-Realization: An Ecological Approach to Being in the World." In *Deep Ecology for the 21st Century: Readings on the Philosophy and Practice of the New Environmentalism*, edited by George Sessions, 225–39. Boston: Shambhala Publications, 1995.

Plotkin, Bill. *Nature and Human Soul: Cultivating Wholeness and Community in a Fragmented World*. Novato, CA: New World Library, 2007.

Plotkin, Bill. *Soulcraft: Crossing into the Mysteries of Nature and Psyche*. Novato, CA: New World Library, 2003.

Plotkin, Bill. *Wild Mind: A Field Guide to the Human Psyche*. Novato, CA: New World Library, 2013.

Roszak, Theodore. *Voice of the Earth: An Exploration of Ecopsychology*. Grand Rapids, MI: Phanes Press, 2001.

Roszak, Theodore, Mary E. Gomes, and Allen D. Kanner, eds. *Ecopsychology: Restoring the Earth, Healing the Mind*. San Francisco: Sierra Books, 1995.

Simon, JH. *How to Kill a Narcissist: Debunking the Myth of Narcissism and Recovering from Narcissistic Abuse*. Self-published, 2016.

Starhawk. *The Earth Path: Grounding Your Spirit in the Rhythms of Nature*. San Francisco: HarperSanFrancisco, 2004.

Twenge, Jean M., and W. Keith Campbell. *The Narcissism Epidemic: Living in the Age of Entitlement*. New York: Atria, 2009.

# INDEX

# ABOUT THE AUTHOR

Jeanine M. Canty, PhD, lives in the foothills above Boulder, Colorado, within the ancestral lands of the Arapaho, Cheyenne, and Ute peoples. She is a professor within the transformative studies doctoral program at the California Institute of Integral Studies (CIIS), and she also guest teaches for Naropa University, Pacifica Graduate Institute, and Prescott College. A lover of nature, justice, and contemplative practice, her teaching intersects issues of social and ecological justice connected to the process of worldview expansion and positive change, and her research situates in ecopsychology, climate justice, transformative learning, contemplative education, and transpersonal inquiries. She is an editor of and a contributor to *Ecological and Social Healing: Multicultural Women's Voices* and *Globalism and Localization: Emergent Approaches to Ecological and Social Crises*. Jeanine is a certified meditation instructor as well as a wilderness first responder (WFR). Her work has been featured in *A Wild Love for the World: Joanna Macy and the Work of Our Time*; *The Wiley Handbook of Transpersonal Psychology*; *The Body and Oppression: Roots, Resistance, and Resolutions*; *Shadows and Light: Principles, Practices, Pedagogy*; and *Multicultural Perspectives of Contemporary Transpersonal Counseling*. Her favorite activities include gardening, yoga, baking pies and pizza, biking for transportation, being in nature, spending time with her loved ones, reading, and, of course, writing.